A PRACTICAL GUIDE TO
PLANTS FOR
PROBLEM
AREAS

A PRACTICAL GUIDE TO
PLANTS FOR
PROBLEM
AREAS

||| •PARRAGON• |||

Introduction

The perfect garden, with well-drained but moisture-retentive, fertile soil and a sunny, sheltered aspect is every gardener's dream. Yet few gardens are like this and most gardeners have specific problems to contend with in their gardens. Such problem areas present an opportunity to exercise skill and judgement in choosing a range of suitable plants or in finding a way to disguise unwanted features. If the soil under trees is bare, dry and shaded, for example, plants that camouflage the ground can be grown. In the same way, plants that unite the topsoil can be planted on a steep slope to help prevent soil erosion.

A soil that is either too acid or too alkaline is a common problem. Though applications of lime can counteract acidity, an alkaline soil is more difficult to correct and it is best to plant lime-loving plants.

Gardening in coastal areas can be particularly difficult. Strong, salt-laden winds damage the surfaces of leaves and hinder the establishment of young plants. By selecting hardy, tolerant plants and establishing windbreaks and hedges early in a garden's life, however, it is possible to overcome some of these problems.

Lack of space can be a gardener's nightmare. Growing summer-bedding plants in pots, window-boxes and hanging-baskets, or dwarf fruit trees, vegetables and herbs in tubs are among the solutions.

This book provides ideas on how to overcome some of the most common gardening problems and shows you how to use the natural characteristics of your garden to your advantage.

© Marshall Cavendish 1995

Some of this material has previously appeared in the
Marshall Cavendish partwork **My Garden**.

CLB 4384

This edition published 1995 by Parragon Book Services Ltd
Unit 13-17 Avonbridge Trading Estate, Atlantic Road
Avonmouth, Bristol BS11 9QD.

ISBN 1-85813-881-7

Printed in Hong Kong

Contents

Types of Soil

For successful, satisfying gardening, you need to know what kind of soil you have and how to make the most of it.

It does not matter whether you are a complete beginner or consider yourself a bit of an expert; unless you know your soil you will never obtain the best results from your garden. Every plant has different preferences – for instance, some thrive on an acid soil while others do not.

Soil is made up of four basic components which are present in varying amounts.

Organic matter is essential to any fertile soil. It is composed of decaying plants and animals and puts back into the soil what the plants have taken out (worms help by pulling leaf litter underground as they tunnel). It is also referred to as humus.

Air is necessary to ensure that the organic matter is broken down and to prevent waterlogging, while **water** carries the nutrients to the plant and clings to the soil particles. Some soils are less able to hold water than others: sand for

The glorious hydrangea (above) is a mixture of colours because the soil is limy and alkaline and is turning the blue hydrangea pink. The hydrangea would be purely blue on an acid soil.

example drains very quickly giving the plant less time to take it up.

Minerals are the rock particles in the soil and they are chiefly responsible for the texture. When these vital components are well balanced good humus results and the soil is healthy and fertile.

Soil texture

The soil is made up of pieces of material of different sizes. A soil which is made from large,

FROM TOP TO BOTTOM

There is usually a distinct difference between the top layer of your soil, the topsoil, and what lies below it, the subsoil. Depending on how well established your garden is and what are the geological qualities of the area, the topsoil may vary from a couple of inches to several feet deep. There may even be a range of different soil types and this can work to your advantage as well as against you. Gravel under clay provides good drainage and chalk under acid neutralises acidity. Take care not to bury the topsoil under the subsoil when digging.

Mike Shoebridge

TOPSOIL

Topsoil (the dark, shaded part of the diagram, left) can vary in depth from a couple of inches to several feet. More open in structure and darker in colour, it is organic material and rich in nutrients. Plants, especially small ones, feed mostly from this layer. Worms are vital because they mix up the material.

SUBSOIL

Lying below the topsoil, subsoil is a less rich layer, providing water and a firm anchorage for larger plants, trees and shrubs.

Eric Crichton

This magnificent scented lilac border flourishes where most plants would flounder. Lilac grows well on thin, starved chalky soils.

Brian Carter/The Garden Picture Library

This aptly named 'Fireglow' azalea is a member of the rhododendron group of plants and, like its relatives, it grows well on acid, peaty soils.

Collection/Patrick Johns

Roses, like this delightful hybrid tea 'Le Havre', grow particularly well on clay soils; although some roses will grow quite happily on sandy soils too.

coarse particles is known as 'light' while a 'heavy' soil is made up of tiny grains. Ideally the composition should be somewhere between the two: a mid-textured soil is known as a loam.

The way soil particles are held together is known as the structure. A clay soil has minute particles which cling together in clumps. Other soils form flat layers or plates, but the best structure is one which is crumbly. This is known as a 'good tilth'. A crumbly loam has the perfect structure and texture but you must also find out how acid or alkaline your soil is in order to decide which plants you will be able to grow. This can be done very cheaply and easily with a soil testing kit. It will only take a few minutes and may save you years of unsuccessful attempts.

Whatever your soil, you will not be able to change either the structure or the acid/alkaline balance completely. But do not despair. Even if you have a heavy clay or a highly alkaline soil you can still improve it enormously. Finding out all you can is the first step.

Basic soil-types

Peat It is rare to find a garden soil that is very peaty, but it does occasionally happen. The area has at some time in the past been wet and boggy, like the fen lands of East Anglia.

Dark in colour, with a light and spongy texture, peaty soils have a high fibrous content – if you squeeze a handful it will fall apart easily.

Peat soils are capable of absorbing and retaining large amounts of water, which they can hold right up to the surface. Drainage can sometimes be a problem but generally it is a soil which is easy to work and very fertile.

This open texture and high moisture content is ideal for growing hydrangeas, rhododendrons, pieris and the many kinds of heathers. Primulas and lilies do well, and so does blue poppy (meconopsis).

All these plants appreciate

CLAY

SAND

CHALK

PEAT

LOAM

	How to recognise	Advantages
CLAY	A heavy, sticky soil. A squeezed handful will stick together and retain its compressed shape.	Usually rich in nutrients. A clay subsoil is ideal for making pond
SAND	Light, crumbly and free-draining. A squeezed handful will fall apart easily.	Fast to warm up in spring. Law will drain freely, and borders ca be worked on all winter if the weather permits. Does not stick to tools.
CHALK	Limy soils vary a great deal, from thin, stony loam over chalk bed to a deep clay soil. But they all have a high pH value (= alkaline).	A moderately limy soil will gro a wide range of plants.
PEAT	A dark, fibrous and spongy soil. A squeezed handful will not hold together. Water may sometimes be squeezed out.	Ideal for acid-loving plants and those which need a high moisture level at all times.
LOAM	Brown or red, medium-weight soil, with plenty of organic matter. A squeezed handful will hold together but can be made to crumble easily.	A loam soil of neutral pH (7) is the ideal soil for growing a wid range of plants, especially vegetables.

sadvantages	Will grow/won't grow
ow to warm up in spring. Lack free drainage is hostile to any kinds of plants. Difficult to eed, and compacts easily in rders and under lawns.	Good for roses, irises and many water-side plants. Unsuitable for rhododendrons, heathers, tenders shrubs, bulbs and alpines.
n be very lacking in nutrients, quiring the addition of much ganic matter and fertilizer. es out quickly, even when lched.	Grows most things, but poor for moisture-loving plants such as many primulas, hostas and bergenias.
ten dry, thin and starved, over ck. Will not support acid-loving nts at all. Some plants come 'chlorotic' (yellow ves).	Good for lilac, cistus and hebes. Bad for most heathers, rhododendrons and hydrangeas.
nstant high moisture level is d for tender/drought-loving nts which need sharp ainage. Lawns can be poor.	Good for rhododendrons, azaleas, heathers, lilies and primulas. Bad for cistus and dianthus. Extra lime needed for good vegetables.
am can be acid or alkaline, and erefore plant choice is limited cordingly.	Alkaline loams will NOT support acid-loving plants.

Peter McHoy

Photos Horticultural

moisture, but some of them, especially those in the heather family, must have another of the qualities of peaty soil: acidity. If a soil is acid, it means it is lacking in lime, a substance which some plants will not tolerate. Soil acidity is measured on the pH scale. Rhododendrons and heathers prefer a pH of about 5-6.5.

Lime Soils containing lime can be very varied. At worst they can be dry, thin and stony, over solid chalk or limestone. But at best they are excellent, rich, loamy soils, which happen to be alkaline.

The only way to be sure whether a soil is alkaline is to test its pH value, and see if it is above pH7.

There are very few limitations of a rich but alkaline soil. It will not grow plants such as rhododendrons, pieris and summer-flowering heathers, because they must have acid soil. But it will grow good roses, vegetables, lawns and an enormous range of flowers and shrubs.

Extreme alkalinity may, however, cause yellowing of the leaves (chlorosis) in some plants such as camellias. Blue-flowered hydrangeas also turn pink on limy soils.

Thin, dry alkaline soils over chalk are more of a problem, and can be very limiting. They tend to be lacking in nutrients and are often stony and difficult to work and are sticky and soft in wet weather. Not all plants flounder on limy soils, some prefer it: cistus, rosemary and carnations (the dianthus family), will be perfectly happy there.

Sand Crumbly and free-draining, sandy soils are without doubt the easiest to work with. Tools keep themselves clean with almost no effort, and the soil warms up quickly in spring which means it is suitable for early crops.

Although this type of soil is good for growing alpines, and shrubs and perennials of doubtful hardiness, the real problem with sand is likely to

GARDEN NOTES

ACIDITY AND ALKALINITY

The term pH (potential of Hydrogen) is a scale for measurement of the chemical alkaline/acidity level of soil. The full scale runs from 1 to 14, but most garden soils are within the range of 4 to 8. When a soil contains enough lime or chalk to give a pH value of over 7, it is said to be alkaline. A pH balance of 6.5 or less is acid. A pH reading of 7 is neutral.

In hot and dry weather, clay will shrink and crack, because of its poor drainage. Plants with shallow root systems such as these dwarf herbaceous plants (top) cannot cope with the extreme conditions that clay produces. Roses or hardy shrubs make a better choice for clay beds.

Rhododendrons are unable to extract vital nutrients from chalky soils, such as this shrub (above), which is showing its suffering with yellowing, or chlorotic, leaves.

TESTING YOUR SOIL

Marshall Cavendish

Soil testing kits can be bought from garden centres and other gardening outlets. They take only minutes to do and can save you years of trial and error in trying to grow the wrong plants on the wrong soil. These kits test the pH value of your soil; pH is simply a scale, ranging from 4–8, which measures the acidity or alkalinity of your soil. The range of 3–6.5 indicates acidity, 7.5–8 alkalinity, 7.0 is neutral.

Remember to test several parts of your garden to get an overall view and if you are treating the soil, test after treatment and compare the results.

A rich, neutral loam is the ideal soil and if you are lucky enough to have it in your garden you will be able to grow practically anything. It has an excellent moisture content and a good crumbly texture. Plenty of organic material ensures that your plants get maximum nutrition, so there is less need to feed. Here it has been used to create a beautiful flower-filled garden.

be dryness. The topsoil, and even the subsoil, can be so free-draining because of its open texture that, in times of drought, thirsty plants will soon wilt for want of a good drink of water and even trees, with their extensive roots may show signs of suffering.

The topsoil, of course, can be made to hold more water by adding some humus to it. Nutritional enrichments – fertilizer – is often necessary, too, in large quantities.

Most plants will grow well on sandy soil but be careful with shallow-rooted varieties.

So long as it is on the acidic side (with a pH value below 7), even summer heathers and rhododendrons thrive. They enjoy the open texture of sandy soils; for your part, give them sufficient water and they will do very well.

Clay Probably the hardest type of soil to deal with. In winter, clay is cold, wet and sticky, so that you cannot work on the garden for fear of compacting the soil into a solid mass. Plants can literally drown when clay soils become waterlogged. In summer, clay can dry out and crack. Because

of poor drainage, the moisture will simply evaporate. It is never easy to weed. Seedling weeds seem to be stuck to the soil in winter and baked on during a dry summer.

Good for roses

Clay soil is not all bad news, however. It can be very fertile, it is well supplied with plant foods, and they are not drained away by a heavy rainfall. Roses grow best of all, along with a good range of shrubs and perennials. And the texture can be improved with effort over the years. It will never make a light, open soil, so it is better to stick to plants which will tolerate clay successfully, rather than try those which will just survive and never look at their best.

Clay soils can be either on the acidic or alkaline side, but generally the lime-loving plants like lilac and cistus do best on it. Often a heavy loam topsoil will be found overlying a clay subsoil, and this is a satisfactory combination.

Loam The ideal soil for gardening, loam will grow much the widest range of plants. It posesses all of the good points of sandy and clay soils but few of their disadvantages. It can be acidic or alkaline, which will limit the choice of plants a little, but, broadly speaking, you can grow anything on loam. Certainly a medium acidic loam will grow rhododendrons perfectly well.

Insight Picture Library

Best of all

The advantage of loam is that it has a high content of organic matter, which is full of nutrients and holds water well. A handful of an average loam, when squeezed, will have enough fibre and moisture to stick together afterwards, but will not be so sticky that you cannot easily make it crumble again.

This is just what growing plants need for healthy foliage and root systems. For vegetables you could not do better.

Gardening on Clay

Clay soils may seem like a serious problem, but properly treated they can be very fertile. To get the very most from them you will need to improve the structure of the soil and grow suitable plants.

Clay soils are characteristically cold, wet and muddy in winter. In summer, they set into hard rocky clods and wide cracks may appear in lawns. But they are easier to 'cure' than you might think.

Coping with clay soil needs a two-pronged attack. In the early stages, it is important to improve the soil; you will probably have to do this gradually in easy stages.

In time, there is no reason why you should not be able to grow almost anything. Improved clay is one of the best gardening soils you could possibly have. Plants growing in it rarely, if ever, suffer from drought – even in long, hot, sunny summers.

Clay's structure

Plants take in water, nutrients and air through their roots. In most soils, which are made up of different particle sizes, there are plenty of air spaces in the soil. But clay soil consists only of tiny particles, which have equally tiny air spaces between them.

This lack of aeration is one of the main reasons why plants have a problem growing in clay. The small particle size also makes clay soils muddy in wet weather; each individual particle is coated with a film of moisture when wet – so wet clay soil holds far more water than an equal volume of wet sandy soil.

Once wet, clay soil stays wet for a long time; water cannot drain away, due to lack of air spaces. To make matters worse, wet clay soil is soft, and is easily compressed if it is walked on, or if you run heavy equipment such as a barrow over it. As a result, plant roots find it difficult to penetrate the hard ground.

Worse still, compressed clay has fewer air spaces than ever, creating conditions in which roots have no oxygen, and rot very easily due to the presence of anaerobic bacteria.

The most frequent advice given for improving clay soils is to add lots of organic matter, such as well rotted manure or garden compost. Certainly clay soils do benefit from organic matter. But because it decomposes so fast, you must add more every year to

Gaping cracks often form in clay soil (below left) especially during the dry, hot summer months. In winter the reverse happens and muddy clods can occur. The 'cure' is to first break down the soil with grit. Plenty of bulky, organic compost (bottom left) can then be added to further improve its quality.

Plants that are especially intolerant of damp, wet clay, such as alpines, will thrive in a raised bed (below).

Ribes laurifolium (below right), which grows well on clay, can benefit from an annual mulching, to conserve surface moisture in summer.

maintain the improvement.

The very best improver for clay soil is coarse gritty sand. (Ask for washed horticultural grit – this can be bought by the bag from garden centres, or, if you need it, in bulk from a builder's merchant.)

Because grit does not break down in the soil one 'treatment' should do. Use about two barrows full of grit per square metre/yard. Spread this roughly over the soil, and dig it in to the top 'spit' (the depth of the blade of a spade).

Once this has been done, any organic matter you can add to the soil will be a further benefit, but you will have definitely made a lasting improvement to the overall physical structure of the soil.

Do not go to enormous efforts trying to dig clay soil. Once you have dug in enough gritty sand to open up the texture, you need never dig it again unless the soil gets firmly compacted.

Improving clay

Organic matter can be added as a mulch (in a layer 2.5-5cm/ 1-2in deep) spread round plants in the spring. This will be pulled down into the soil by worms. By replenishing the mulch every spring, the organic level in the soil will rise without effort on your part.

Hoeing, planting and pulling out old plants all help to incorporate organic matter into the soil without digging.

Clay soils are best cultivated fairly shallowly – certainly never more than a spit deep –

due to the presence of infertile subsoil below the surface. If you dig a hole you will often see greasy blue or yellowish clay. This should never be brought to the surface as nothing will grow in it for many years, even if it is mixed with grit and organic matter.

If you take on a new garden where subsoil has been turned up by building work, it is best removed. Buy in good topsoil rather than try to work with clay subsoil.

Trees and shrubs

When planting trees or shrubs, do not just dig a deep hole and put compost at the bottom, as you would on lighter soils. If you do, the planting hole acts as a sump, filling up with water and drowning the plant roots.

Instead, improve the soil over the whole bed by digging in a mixture of grit and organic matter to one spade's depth. This encourages plants to form

Tania Midgley

Collections/Patrick Johns

GARDEN NOTES

DIGGING CLAY

Avoid digging clay soil when it is either very hard and cloddy in summer or too wet and muddy in winter. Not only is it hard work, but you risk damaging the soil structure.

There is a short time when clay is in a workable condition in autumn, shortly after the first serious rain. If you do not dig then, sowing and planting will be delayed, as clay soils are slow to dry out in spring.

Cover the ground with cloches or sheets of black polythene for two to three weeks before sowing or planting. This gives the soil a chance to dry out and warm up. It is vital for early sowings, as seed often rots if conditions are poor.

Always work from a plank when sowing or planting, to avoid compacting the soil.

a wide ranging root system which has a mixture of both shallow and deep roots.

Mulch trees and shrubs every spring, especially notoriously shallow rooting kinds such as rhododendron. This not only adds organic matter to the soil, but also conserves moisture near the surface in summer, preventing soil from cracking. (As soil shrinks, it strips off the fine root hairs and this can cause serious problems.) Mulching also insulates roots from heat and cold.

Beds and borders

Improve surface drainage by building beds up slightly above the level of the surrounding lawn. Use low retaining walls if necessary. In this way, plants grow in well drained soil, but their roots will be able to reach moisture reserves held by clay situated further down.

Plants that particularly need well drained conditions, such as Mediterranean plants, pinks and those with silver leaves, will need extra grit mixed with the soil, to prevent roots rotting in winter.

Always mulch between border plants each spring to retain moisture and maintain soil improvement. And as a precaution against rotting on unimproved clay, be sure to work a few handfuls of grit in among the crowns of herbaceous plants in autumn.

Fruit

Most fruit trees and bushes need reasonably well drained soil. Only blackcurrants and blackberries tolerate unimproved clay. Other soft fruit do best in the vegetable garden in raised beds.

Fruit trees are best trained as fans, cordons or espaliers and grown up against a wall — this soaks up some of the surplus moisture in winter. Mulch plants well in spring to retain as much soil moisture as possible in summer.

Most books recommend

PLANTS THAT THRIVE ON CLAY

Trees
Acer
Amelanchier lamarckii
Birches
Eucalyptus
Hawthorn
Laburnum
Malus
Prunus
Salix
Sorbus

Shrubs
Aucuba
Berberis
Chaenomeles
Choisya ternata
Cornus alba
Corylus avellana 'Contorta'
Cotoneaster
Escallonia
Forsythia
Hypericum
Kerria japonica
Philadelphus
Pyracantha
Rhododendron
Ribes
Roses
Spiraea
Symphoricarpos
Syringa
Weigela

Climbers
Clematis
Jasminum nudiflorum (winter jasmine)
Lonicera (honeysuckle)

Hedging
Hawthorn
Hornbeam
Privet

Herbaceous
Alchemilla mollis (lady's mantle)
Anemone japonica (Japanese anemone)
Artemisia absinthium 'Lambrook Silver'
Bergenia
Epimedium perralderianum, *E. × rubrum*
Geranium species
Hosta
Ligularia
Lysimachia nummularia
Kniphofia
Peony
Polygonatum × hybridum (Solomon's seal)
Pulmonaria (lungwort)
Ranunculus acris 'Flore Pleno', *R. repens* 'Flore Pleno' (double buttercups)
Thalictrum aquilegiifolium,

T. dipterocarpum 'Hewitt's Double'
Tricyrtis (toad lily)

Grasses and ferns
Adianthum venustum (hardy maidenhair fern)
Asplenium scolopendrium (hart's tongue fern)
Miscanthus sacchariflorus, *M. sinensis*
Phalaris arundinacea 'Picta'

Flowers
Euphorbia characias wulfenii
Gentiana acaulis, *G. septemfida*
Helleborus orientalis, *H. foetidus*
Iris foetidissima
Liriope muscari
Polyanthus
Primroses
Verbascum bombyciferum

Bulbs
Allium sphaerocephalon
A. cernuum, A. siculum
Cyclamen hederifolium
Daffodils/narcissi
Lilium martagon, *L. pyrenaicum*
Snowdrops

Karin Craddock/Garden Picture Library

Very popular for its aromatic and silvery-grey foliage, the **Eucalyptus gunnii** *(left) grows well on clay soils but requires shelter from strong winds in winter.*

The striking **Tricyrtis stoloniferia** *(toad lily) needs humus-rich, moist soil to flourish (above right) and brings late summer or autumn colour to the garden.*

*Add a flash of colour with these unusually blue flowers (above far right) of the hardy gentian (***Gentiana acaulis***). It is an excellent choice for clay beds.*

This hardy, summer-flowering bulb, **Allium sphaerocephalon** *(right) also prefers to grow in clay and in a good year may produce as many as 40 ball-shaped, pinkish to purple coloured flowers.*

Andrew Lawson

Derek Gould

Photos Horticultural

installing land drains before laying a lawn on clay soil. But this is far too expensive for most people. It is also no use unless the water has somewhere to drain away.

Lawns

A more practical solution is to dig in plenty of grit and organic matter when preparing the soil before sowing or turfing a lawn. If you can raise the level of the ground up even an inch or two above that of the surrounding land, you will have enough surface drainage to make the difference between a good and bad lawn.

If the grass is already established, you can still improve the soil beneath it. Every autumn, top dress the whole lawn with horticultural grit, or a mixture of grit and topsoil or sieved garden compost. Spike the lawn and work the top dressing into the grass with a stiff brush or the back of a rake.

If the lawn cracks open in dry spells in summer, take the opportunity to brush more of the grit mixture into the fissures. As the soil structure improves, it stops cracking.

Bulbs

Few bulbs grow really happily in wet, heavy, clay soils. Daffodils and narcissi are probably the most tolerant.

On clay, bulbs are best grown in a shrub border. The shrubs draw all the available moisture from the soil in summer, when the bulbs need to be dry. Even so, it is a good idea to plant them on top of a few handfuls of grit, for extra drainage in winter.

If you want to grow bulbs that are distinctly intolerant of winter wet – such as tulips or lilies – choose a raised bed in a sunny part of the garden. Crown Imperials, which have hollow tops to their bulbs, should be planted lying on their sides, so water cannot gather in them and make them rot.

Alternatively, plant difficult bulbs in pots. Keep them in a cold frame or unheated greenhouse in winter to protect them from damp, and plunge the pots in the garden in spring, when the soil is drier.

Rock plants

Alpines are the most difficult plants of all to grow on clay, as they easily rot in wet soil – especially in winter.

Raised beds are essential. In place of a conventional rockery, you could however grow them on a bank, or in a scree bed (basically a raised bed filled with a very open gritty soil, covered by gravel).

Using one of these three alternatives, your plants, many of which send roots long distances in search of moisture, will be able to reach water without sitting in it.

Acid-loving Plants

In most gardens, the soil type dictates which plants will thrive and which will fail. Here's how to make the most of a garden with acid soil.

Gillian Beckett

Gardening without understanding your soil is like cooking without any temperature controls. You will only learn by trial and error after many dishes have been burnt. Similarly with soil – if you do not know your soil type many plants will die and a great deal of effort and money wasted before you discover the best plants for your garden. Once you know the facts, the door to successful gardening will be opened for you and you can buy plants which will flourish year after year.

If you discover that your soil is acid you will be amazed by the possibilities. Far from being limited by your soil it should encourage you to use suitable plants more creatively. Rhododendrons, azaleas and heathers are ericaceous, which means they thrive on acid soils and perish on soils which are limy and alkaline.

You can often tell at a glance whether the soil in your area is acid. If there are lots of thriving rhododendrons around (above) there is a good chance that it will be but do a soil test to make sure. Guesswork may prove expensive and frustrating. This sad-looking peony (right) has become chlorotic (its leaves have turned yellow) because it has been grown on chalky soil.

Peter McHoy

If acid-loving plants are grown on an alkaline soil they soon become yellow (chlorotic) and sickly. Depending upon the plants and the degree of lime in the soil, they can either die quite quickly or linger on for years looking miserable and worthless. This is because some of the nutrients in the soil, particularly iron, are bound up by the lime and are made unavailable to acid-loving plants. Without these nutrients, the plants slowly starve to death.

Know your soil

The first thing to do is to test the pH value of the soil. Very often you can tell quickly just by looking in the neighbouring gardens whether the soil in your district is acid. If there are lots of rhododendrons and heathers there is a good chance it will be, but it is still worth testing.

You may find that, while most of your garden is acidic, there is limy soil around the house walls, or that an old vegetable patch has been heavily limed. Do test your soil first, so as to give your new and expensive plants the best possible chance of survival.

Test kits are inexpensive and are available from all garden centres, nurseries, and some department stores. The pH scale measures acidity and alkalinity. A reading of 7 is neutral. Below that it is acidic, and the likelihood is that an acidic garden soil will be in the range of pH5-6.5, which is fine for acid-loving plants.

Only very rarely do you find soil with a reading lower than pH5. A pH reading of about 7 means the soil is unsuitable for lime-hating (calcifuge) plants. If your soil is close to pH7, however, it may be worth trying to acidify pockets of soil in the garden which will enable you to grow acid-lovers. If the reading is above pH8, however, it is not worth the effort and expense. It is far better to garden within the natural limitations of your soil.

Improving your soil

In trying to improve a soil to make it suitable for acid-loving plants, it is worth remembering that there are other qualities of acid soils

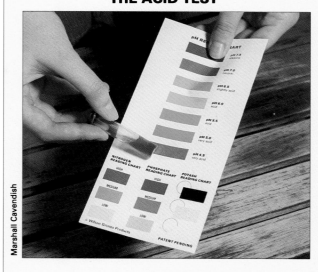

THE ACID TEST

Marshall Cavendish

To be sure of the acidity or alkalinity of your soil, test the pH value. A value of about 5-6.5 is ideal for acid loving plants. The soil must be below 7 as the soil above 6.5 is too limy.

which also need to be sought after and encouraged.

The first of these qualities is an open texture. Most acid soils tend to be peaty or sandy, and they usually have a crumbly texture which contains plenty of air. Think of the crumbly leaf mould on the floor of an oak wood. Indeed, acid leaf mould, which you can

If your soil is limy you can still grow acid-loving plants in containers. Use a proprietary compost which has the correct acid balance and all the nutrients the plants will need. The rich colour of the hydrangea (below) assures you that it is not suffering from any mineral deficiency.

ERICACEOUS COMPOSTS

Ericaceous is the gardening term for plants in the erica, or heather, family and most other acid-loving plants. If you intend to grow acid-loving plants such as azaleas or small rhododendrons in containers, perhaps because your garden soil is alkaline and the lime would damage them, then use a proprietary ericaceous compost. It is far superior to a peat and grit mixture because it also has all the nutrients necessary for sustained growth which are lacking in peat alone.

Acid-loving plants hate a rich compost, but need minerals to survive.

GARDEN NOTES

Photos Horticultural

CLASSIC PLANTS FOR ACID SOILS

At first glance the new red leaves of this pieris look almost like flowers.

Kalmia angustifolia 'Rubra' is a bushy shrub with clusters of deep pink flowers.

The bright blue star-shaped flowers of lithospermum are produced in profusion.

- Rhododendron species and hybrids vary from 15cm/6in to 3.6m/12ft high. Most flower in the spring.

- Azaleas, part of the rhododendron family, come in two main kinds: Kurume azaleas are evergreen, flower in early spring and grow to a height of 30-60cm/1-2ft; deciduous azaleas flower in late spring and grow to a height of 75cm-2.1m/2½ft-7ft.

- Camellias flower mainly in early spring and grow to a height of 1.5m-2.1m/5-7ft. They require a sheltered position to flower well.

- Pieris are attractive evergreen shrubs with a lily-of-the-valley type flower and beautifully coloured new foliage.

- Magnolias prefer a deep, humus-rich soil.

- Hydrangeas are best in a moist, rich soil, sheltered from cold winds. They do well near the sea. Hydrangeas will grow on lime, but too much makes them chlorotic and alters the colour of the flowers from blue to pink.

- Eucryphia is a small group of narrow, mostly evergreen trees suitable for the smaller garden. The attractive white flowers, like single roses, appear in late summer and early autumn.

- The snowdrop tree (*Styrax japonica*) is a shrub or small tree with masses of white 'snowdrops' hanging from the branches in early summer.

- Enkianthus is an attractive group of slow-growing shrubs carrying coppery bells in late spring and followed by excellent autumn colour. These grow to 1.8-2.4m/6-8ft.

- Calico bush (*Kalmia Latifolia*), is a medium sized evergreen shrub with clusters of deep pink-red flowers in early summer.

- Fothergilla, a group of small spring-flowering shrubs, have white bottle-brush flowers followed by attractive autumn colours.

- Pernettya, small but spreading evergreen shrubs, are grown for their colourful berries. Male and female plants are needed to produce berries.

- Gaultheria is a group of (mainly) small creeping evergreens with bright autumn berries.

- Leucothoe, small shrubs for shade, have arching evergreen stems and attractive foliage. The form 'Rainbow' has leaves of cream, yellow and pink.

- Willows include species with very attractive foliage, stems and catkins.

- *Cornus canadensis* is a good small carpeting shrub for moist shade. The stems bear starry white flowers. It is slow to establish.

- Heathers are colourful, low evergreens requiring an open peaty soil and full light. They flower in early spring and autumn.

- Lithospermum is a beautiful sprawling shrub which looks particularly well amongst heathers. The flowers are produced from late spring and are a most vivid blue. Look for the varieties 'Grace Ward' and 'Heavenly Blue'.

- The blue poppy, Meconopsis, is a perennial plant with stunning flowers which it produces in late spring and early summer. In warm areas pick a cool spot for planting.

make yourself by composting leaves, is the ideal additive for improving your soil. It is far better than peat because it contains more nutrients.

Alternatively, well-rotted garden compost will do, as long as it is not too rich. Green peat can be bought conveniently and easily, but it is definitely second best and, as it is a limited resource, it should be used only where necessary.

Sand, grit or pine needles can be used to open up the texture of heavier soils. Do make sure that you use sand that is not alkaline, though. Builder's sand, for example, can often be very limy.

Keep it moist

The second quality needed by acid-loving plants is adequate drainage and a good moisture content. If your soil is acidic and sandy, you will need to add as much organic matter to the soil as possible in order to build up the humus content and help to retain moisture.

Use anything you can get hold of, from leaf mould and

CARE OF ACID-LOVING PLANTS

Your tap water, which probably contains far too much lime, may not be suitable for watering acid-lovers. Lime-free rainwater is a far better bet. Collect it in a water butt, if you have room for one.

If plants become chlorotic (yellow), use Sequestrene in diluted or powder form, following the manufacturer's directions carefully.

Brian Carter/Garden Picture Library

A water butt collects rainwater which will be suitable for most acid-loving plants.

Marshall Cavendish

Apply diluted Sequestrene to the roots of large plants, using a watering can.

Marshall Cavendish

If a smaller plant is suffering sprinkle dry Sequestrene on the roots and water in.

Acid soils tend to be peaty or sandy and they usually have an open texture which acid-loving plants are particularly fond of. To enhance the texture of your soil make a mulch of well rotted acid leaves, pine needles or ordinary garden compost and apply it annually around the base of your plants (above). This will also improve the drainage and moisture content of the soil.

A raised bed is an ideal home for acid-loving plants in a limy garden. Make a wall with bricks, stones or even peat blocks and fill it with acid components such as grit, acid loam soil and garden compost. It need not be as big as the grand example (left), but the effect you will achieve can be just as spectacular.

compost to peat. It will all help. Dig plenty in before you plant, and be prepared to mulch the soil annually.

Self-contained

One way of growing acid lovers on an alkaline soil is to use raised beds or containers. Containers filled with ericaceous compost remain permanently acidic – and camellias in tubs can look wonderful in a courtyard. They will need gentle feeding over the years, however, and they will need soft water at all times. If your tap water is limy (look for scale in the kettle) then you will need to collect rainwater for your acid containers.

A simpler solution is to create raised beds of acid soil on top of your existing garden soil. These will naturally stay much damper than containers because of contact with the ground.

Raised beds

Raised beds can be made using low walls of brick or stone (not limestone of course) or even with peat blocks. To be successful a depth of not less than 25cm/10in is required. Fill your beds with a mixture of whatever acid components you can find or afford. Grit, leafmould, garden compost, acid loam soil or peat will all be suitable for this.

Over the years worms will tend to bring up lime into the

acid soil, but periodic topdressings of leaf mould or peat will help to keep up acidity.

Chemical solutions

The use of Sequestrene may also be beneficial. This is a chemical powder which is diluted with water and is then watered onto the soil around plants which show signs of lime intolerance. It simply makes the lacking minerals directly available to the plants. In this form these elements cannot be 'pinched' by the lime in the soil. The benefits can be dramatic, but it is an expensive way of helping lime-hating plants, and should be used only in addition to basic soil improvement.

Over-acidity can be conveniently corrected by the application of lime. Spread it on the soil surface in winter and simply allow the rain and frost to dig it in for you.

HERBACEOUS ACID LOVERS

GARDEN NOTES

Many popular border plants will happily grow on an acid soil, giving plenty of scope for colour-scheming. Choose from the following: Lilies, shooting star, dog's-tooth violet, fritillary or chequered lily, toad lily, astilbe, blue poppy, gentian, false spikenard, blood root and ferns.

Gardening on Chalky Soil

Many of the country's best gardens are on limy soil. You can grow wonderful plants, so long as you bear in mind a few limitations and garden accordingly.

Limy soils are usually found in areas where the rock beneath the surface is composed of chalk or limestone. However, certain sands, especially near coastal areas, are also alkaline; this is because they contain the remnants of sea shells which, like chalk, are composed mainly of calcium. Because calcium produces an alkaline reaction, such soils are generally referred to as 'alkaline' soils.

In limy areas you may, nevertheless, find pockets of topsoil that are neutral or even acid, especially at the bottom of a valley where the depth of soil is usually greater than on the hills.

The alkalinity or acidity of the soil determines which plants grow well and which

Harry Smith Collection

PLANTS TO AVOID

Some plants become chemically starved when grown in a limy soil, and quickly turn yellow and die. They include:
Rhododendrons
Azaleas
Camellias
Pieris
Heathers, including
  Calluna vulgaris
  Erica cinerea
  Erica arborea
  Daboecia cantabrica
and their varieties
Kalmia
Lithospermum
Perenettya
Gaultheria
Cornus kousa
Enkianthus

DON'T FORGET!

Peter McHoy

MEASURING ALKALINITY

The pH scale, from 0-14, is a register of acidity and alkalinity. pH7 is chemically neutral, but 6.5 is regarded as neutral for most plants. pH test kits are available quite cheaply from all garden centres.

You must remember it is not a proportional scale. One step on the pH scale, say from pH6 to pH7, represents a ten-fold increase in alkalinity or acidity. Garden soils usually fall in the range 4-8.5.

If your soil has a pH value of 7.5 or above, your garden is alkaline enough to cause problems for some plants, so choose accordingly.

If you are new to an area and unsure of what type of soil awaits you, the best indicator is always to look at neighbouring gardens, to see what grows there. If the soil is acidic, someone is certain to be growing rhododendrons or heathers. If not, then the chances are you are on an area of limy soil, but test it to be sure.

Whether your soil is thin or, as here, deep and rich, it pays to dig in humus (above). Organic material will make clay easier to work and will increase the depth of thin soil.

Junipers (opposite) will cope with a variety of soils. Some thrive on thin chalky soils.

languish unhappily. Fortunately, though, the majority of garden plants will grow well in both acid and alkaline soils.

Lime and plants

An excessively alkaline soil interferes with the ability of certain plants to take up nutrients. Even though an element like iron, vital for the production of chlorophyll, may be present in the soil, it becomes 'locked' in a form unavailable to some plants.

Those plants that cannot extract the necessary nutrients for healthy growth are called 'calcifuge', or lime-hating, plants. Rhododendrons and pieris, which are adapted to growing on acid soils, are well known lime-haters.

Many plants, such as lilac and carnations, however, have evolved so that they can make the most of the available nutrients. These lime-loving plants are known as 'calcicoles'.

Although most plants will grow well on most soils, they may struggle in very acid or very alkaline conditions. If you have a chalky soil it makes sense to grow plants that thrive in alkaline soils.

Limy soils vary greatly in quality, irrespective of their liminess. There are rich, deep, alluvial, limy soils which grow superb crops and support marvellous gardens. In England, for instance, there are also the cold, limy clays of Kent and Cambridgeshire, the thinner upland soils of the Yorkshire Dales, which lie over limestone hills, and the meagre scraping of stony soil over the chalk Downs. Some are difficult to garden on, but not just because they are limy. It is more to do with the type of soil, its depth and whether it is free-draining or wet.

Improving the soil

It is the poor, thin, limy soils which are the hardest to garden on. Often they are stony, and there is so much lime in the soil that the pH value is very high. It is not really possible to reduce the pH value significantly, and you must garden with it, rather than against it.

You can, though, improve the volume and quality of the soil by adding to it bulky, humus-rich soil conditioners. Compost and well-rotted man-

HYDRANGEA COLOUR

Peter McHoy

Peter McHoy

The colour of the flowers of Hydrangea macrophylla is altered by the pH of the soil. On acid soils (above left) the blooms are blue or purple. On neutral or alkaline soils with a pH greater than 5.5 the blooms will be pink or red (above right). The species shown here is Hydrangea macrophylla 'Deutschland'. Adding colourants will make flowers bluer.

Peter McHoy

PLANTS FOR THIN SOIL

The following plants grow well on thin soil over chalk:
Aucuba
Berberis
Buddleia
Buxus
Ceanothus
Cistus
Cotoneaster
Deutzia
Euonymus
Forsythia
Fuchsia
Hebe
Hypericum
Ligustrum
Lonicera
Mahonia
Philadelphus
Potentilla
Rosa
Rosmarinus
Sambucus
Senecio
Spartium
Syringa
Vinca
Weigela
Yucca

GARDEN NOTES

ure are best. If you can get them cheaply, rotted straw, spent mushroom compost, spent hops or anything similar will do. Spent mushroom compost, however, contains ground limestone, so it will not make your ground any less alkaline, though it well help to improve the soil structure.

Dig in generous amounts whenever you start a new border, or whenever you put in a new plant. And meanwhile, mulch regularly and thickly, letting the worms do the work of pulling the goodness down into the soil.

Mulching is important, too, because it helps keep the soil moist. Thin, stony soils dry out very quickly, which can be damaging to plants.

Growing calcifuges

It is possible to grow lime-hating plants, such as rhododendron and pieris, in limy areas by creating special conditions for them. Tubs or raised beds filled with acid soil or ericaceous compost will work up to a point, but there are problems with them.

In the case of raised beds, worms will eventually bring lime up from the natural underlying soil into your acidic soil. Tubs need an ample supply of soft, acid rainwater. Otherwise you will simply be watering lime onto them when you use alkaline tapwater.

Even if you garden on acid soil your tapwater may be alkaline because it has been piped from a limy area. If your kettle is full of scale, beware. Collect rainwater for your tubs and raised beds.

In time of drought, it is better to give limy water than no water at all. One or two small doses of limy water will not do any great harm.

Plants for limy soil

Rhododendrons and heathers may be non-starters on limy soil, but there are many other plants which grow best on lime. The only limitations will be the soil's other qualities, such as depth, fertility, moisture retentiveness and so on.

Most herbaceous plants do well on limy soil, and the choice there is endless.

Alpines do well, too. You can make a virtue of necessity and make a limestone scree garden, growing small cushion plants through white limestone chippings. Again the choice of plants is endless. You may already have a rockery made of weathered limestone. This will provide an interesting variety of situations for alpines and small perennials.

Most conifers grow happily enough on limy soil. This is true for full-sized specimens and dwarfs. Although you cannot make a traditional heather-and-conifer garden on lime, you can certainly make a collection of dwarf conifers and underplant them with lime-tolerant carpeters. Try using *Polygonum affine* (now more correctly called *Persicaria affine)*, *Geum montanum, Dryas octopetala* and many others.

You can even grow several more lime-tolerant, winter-flowering heathers, such as *Erica carnea* (also sold as *E. herbacea*) and its varieties, so long as you are working with an open-textured soil.

A mulch of large river or seashore pebbles makes an attractive foil to the shapes of mixed conifers. Junipers are especially good on limy soil, and come in many habits, from

Senecio 'Sunshine' (above) is a bushy evergreen shrub with silvery-grey leaves that become dark green. It does well on poor limy soils. The yellow flowers appear in summer.

Artemisia 'Powis Castle' (below) has finely cut silvery-grey foliage and insignificant yellowish-grey flowers.

Photos Horticultural

Joanne Pavia/Garden Picture Library

TREES TO GROW ON CHALK

Shallow soils over chalk can be difficult for trees, not just because of alkalinity, but because of the problems of stability. Not all trees will stand properly without a tap root into deep soil. The following trees are happy over solid chalk:
Ash
Beech
Hornbeam
Horse chestnut
Japanese flowering
  cherry
Norway maple
Sycamore
Hawthorn
Whitebeam

Rosemary (above right), a lovely Mediterranean shrub accustomed to growing on dry, impoverished soils, will thrive on thin soils over lime. Leaves can be used in the kitchen.

Japanese flowering cherries (below) cope with all but waterlogged soils. This weeping variety is Prunus 'Kiku-shidare Sakaru'.

Photos Horticultural

tall and upright to dwarf and prostrate, and in colours ranging from green to blue.

Thin soils

Poor soils over lime are good for growing the slightly tender Mediterranean shrubs, such as lavender, rosemary, cistus, halimium and *Genista hispanica*. This can produce a wonderfully exotic effect in a poor, dry area which is also sunny and sheltered. Many of these plants have aromatic leaves, which will scent the air on warm evenings. They also flower generously in summer.

Grey plants can be mixed with them. Try growing the curry plant (*Helichrysum italicum*, often sold under the name *H. angustifolium*), which will really spice the air, even during the day. *Senecio* 'Sunshine' has yellow flowers over paddle-shaped grey leaves. Cotton lavender (*Santolina neapolitana*) has little, bright yellow, button flowers. The flowers are paler in the form 'Sulphurea'.

Euphorbia characias wulfenii, often sold simply as *E. wulfenii*, is an upright, shrubby spurge, with grey-green leaves and great cylinders of lime-green flowers.

Artemisia 'Powis Castle' will make a silvery mound of beautiful feathery foliage, 1m/3ft across. In a damper position, *Artemisia abrotanum*, or lad's love, can be used for its delightful aromatic foliage. Keep it by a path where you can pinch it as you pass. It will grow to 1.2m/4ft in height and produce yellow flowers.

Heavy soils

On a heavy alkaline soil roses of all kinds grow extremely well and appreciate some gutsy clay down below. Lilac enjoys an alkaline soil that is rich and heavy. A strong, well-fed lilac is as perfumed as any plant and picks beautifully.

Climbing and shrubby honeysuckles are at home on lime. So are the various species of clematis, as long as there is a good depth of soil.

Shrubs

Many shrubs are happy on lime. Philadelphus, deutzia and weigela all do well. The viburnums enjoy lime, and so do buddleia, pyracantha, box, spotted laurel, flowering currant, hazel, berberis, cotoneaster and hypericum.

Hydrangeas can be grown if the soil is not too limy, but it is difficult to achieve those marvellous blue colours. You will need to regularly use artificial colourants.

All the usual hedging plants are suitable for growing on limy soil. Yew, particularly, can be used with success on shallow chalky soils.

Coping with Dry Soil

A dry soil need not be a problem – it can even have its advantages. Get the best out of yours, whether it's naturally dry or has become so in a drought.

Harry Smith Collection

If your soil is permanently dry, do not despair. There is plenty you can do to improve it and all the solutions are easy, if a little time-consuming. Most apply not only to naturally dry soils but also to those which lack moisture in a long, hot summer when there is no rain forecast and hosepipe bans make watering difficult.

The good and the bad

You may have to water a dry soil more often than one that retains water and you may have to add large quantities of compost, but dry soils can have their advantages, too.

For instance, many tender plants require especially good drainage to get them through a cold winter and a dry soil can offer this. Dry, light soils warm up quickly in spring, too, to give you a slightly longer growing season.

No one wants to have to water the garden any more than is really necessary – and water is an increasingly valuable resource. To reduce watering you need to increase the soil's ability to hold the water

it receives naturally. To do this it needs extra organic matter – lots and lots of compost, manure, leaf mould or other bulky, fibrous additives.

Hungry soil

Dry soils tend to be free-draining, which means that they lose nutrients. A dry soil is therefore also a hungry soil. For this reason, when adding bulk to your soil, manure or a good, rich compost will be much more beneficial than peat, which holds water but has no nutritional value.

A lush, green lawn is every gardener's dream, and a careful programme of feeding, weeding and watering is the way to achieve it. Using a lawn sprinkler (above) is the ideal way to give your lawn a good soak – important in a long, dry spell or when a new lawn has just been laid. Do not forget to move the sprinkler occasionally during watering so that the spray can reach every corner of the lawn and no part risks becoming waterlogged.

24

For best results, incorporate your compost into the top two spits of soil (that is, to a depth of about 50cm/20in) before you plant. In a new border this is easy to do but in an established border you will have to treat small areas.

Marvellous mulching

A good mulch of compost around plants will not only seal moisture into the soil by insulating it from wind and sun, it will also provide a banquet for the worms; they will draw it down into the topsoil, taking all the extra nutrients down with it.

A 7.5cm/3in layer of compost in spring is the best start a plant can have on a dry soil. If you are short of compost use leaf mould or well-rotted manure. Spent hops and old mushroom compost are also useful and easy to apply. Bark mulch will help to insulate the soil but it has no nutritional value, while, conversely, concentrated manures, available in bags from garden centres, are full of nutrients but lack the sheer bulk that is needed to enrich a poor, dry soil.

Sandy soils especially need this bulk to improve texture. When such soils have been well composted over a number of years they can be wonderfully deep and fertile.

Chalk and gravel

Soils of mainly chalk or gravel are more difficult and slower to improve. You may have to literally build up a good soil depth over a number of years by adding more and more mulch each spring. There are no short cuts but after a few years you will be pleasantly surprised: your efforts will be rewarded by a richer and more manageable soil. Do not stop mulching, however, or the soil will revert and your efforts will have been wasted.

To keep soil well insulated, plant ground-covering plants. This does not mean crowding shrubs together but it does

WHAT IS DRY SOIL?

A naturally dry soil is any soil with a light texture, containing insufficient organic matter to retain enough moisture. But even a soil that is normally moisture-retentive can become dry during a long hot summer when there is very little rain.
Typical dry soils include:
● **sandy soils** which can be good for many different plants but are often very hungry and may also be acidic
● **chalk soils** which tend to be stony, are very alkaline and need regular generous dressings of compost to improve their fertility

Collections/Patrick Johns

Mulching is one way of conserving moisture around established plants – and, as an extra bonus, it will also help to smother weeds and so cut down on the amount of work you have to do in the garden. Here (right), an Elaeagnus × ebbingei 'Limelight' has been mulched with a layer of shredded bark. Unlike manure or compost, however, bark will not feed the soil at all.

Collections/Patrick Johns

It is very important that young plants like this viburnum (above) receive adequate water. Watering well with a can directly around the base of the plant ensures that the roots are thoroughly moistened.

If you have a new plot or unplanted border, you can really get to grips with improving the soil. Working across the plot, digging a series of trenches which you then fill with manure a number of years (below), is an excellent way of building up a more fertile soil.

IMPROVING DRY SOIL

● Add organic matter to increase the soil's ability to hold moisture naturally. Compost or manure will add valuable nutrients as well as hold water.
● Spread a mulch – a layer of organic matter – around plants to seal moisture into the soil. Again, compost or manure is best as earthworms will gradually draw this down into the soil.
● Grow ground-cover plants to shade the soil.
● Water thoroughly to promote good, deep root growth. Watering little and often will encourage shallow roots, which will be more vulnerable to moisture loss near the surface.

Marshall Cavendish

Marshall Cavendish

Whether your soil is permanently dry, or you are preparing for a dry summer, apply a mulch to a well-watered soil (above). Pay special attention to watering plants close to a wall as these receive less rain.

A seepage hose (below) delivers a small, steady flow of water through tiny holes. Devices are available which control the flow so you can go out without worrying that you will return to a flooded garden. Evening is the best time to water.

Photos Horticultural

mean never leaving large expanses of bare soil.

Choose plants that positively enjoy dry conditions. A plant which is at home on your soil will always look better than one that is visibly struggling to survive.

There is a wider choice of plants for sunny spots in dry soil than there are plants suitable for dry shade.

Chemical remedies

Desperate circumstances do sometimes require quite desperate remedies and there is a substance available to provide a reservoir of water in the soil. Polymer gels, available in granular form from some garden centres, can be an excellent aid in establishing trees and shrubs on dry soils and means they need less watering.

You simply have to mix the dry granules into the bottom of the planting hole. When you water in your new plant the granules swell – like wallpaper paste – and form tiny pockets of moist gel. These act as reservoirs in the soil, from which thirsty roots can obtain water in times of drought.

Heatwaves

There are times when every garden is dry. In a summer

Photos Horticultural

heatwave it is frustrating to watch the beauty you have worked to create and nurture frying to a crisp in the hot sun.

The best advice is to be prepared for a sudden change in the weather. Use mulches just as you would in a permanently dry garden. Even in midsummer, a good mulch put down over well-soaked soil will help to keep the soil quite cool and moist. Do not, however, put a mulch onto a parched soil as it will then act like a sponge, soaking up the first rain before it reaches the plants' roots.

When you do water your garden, do it generously but sensibly. Use a watering can to top up thirsty plants like clematis once a week, whatever the weather. This keeps the plants strong enough to cope during dry spells.

A hand-held hose is usually more effective than a sprinkler, except on lawns. A soil that has only had its surface dampened by a sprinkler will draw up the thirsty roots. Sprinklers can also cause

Brian Carter/The Garden Picture Library

PLANT CHOICE

For sunny spots with dry soil pick from the following:-
- **Shrubs:** brooms (cytisus and genista), cotton lavender (santolina), smoke bush (cotinus), spotted laurel (aucuba), rock rose (helianthemum), senecio, yucca, lavender, rosemary, halimium, hebe, sun rose (cistus).
- **Herbaceous plants:** bearded iris, bear's breeches (acanthus), sea holly (eryngium), cranesbill (geranium), ice plant (sedum), snow-in-summer (cerastium), penstemon, sempervivum, carnations and pinks (dianthus).

For shady spots in dry soil, any of the following plants are a good choice.
- **Shrubs:** spotted laurel (aucuba), box (buxus), *Daphne pontica,* false castor oil plants (fatsia), ivies, rose of Sharon *(Hypericum calycinum),* holly (ilex), privet (ligustrum), *Mahonia aquifolium,* cherry laurel *(Prunus laurocerasus)* and snowberry (symphoricarpos).
- **Herbaceous plants:** bergenia, brunnera, foxglove (digitalis), honesty (lunaria), Solomon's seal (polygonatum), lungwort (pulmonaria), comfrey (symphytum), periwinkle *(Vinca minor),* waldsteinia, *Euphorbia robbiae* and *Iris foetidissima.*

If you have a dry soil or live in an area which is prone to seasonal drought it is wise to select plants which thrive in these conditions. Prunus laurocerasus (above) is ideal for a shady spot while Cytisus nigricans (below) is perfect if you want to fill a sunny area with vibrant colour.

Marshall Cavendish

Marshall Cavendish

leaves to burn when the hot sun shines on them. It is much better to use a hosepipe, directing a gentle flow of water at the root of each thirsty plant. In this way you will channel the water where it is most needed.

Slow but steady

As an alternative to a hand-held hose, a seep hose is effective for watering a border. Like a leaky pipe, a seep hose will deliver a small but steady supply of water through a series of tiny holes. Devices are available to switch off the water when the required volume has been delivered.

Water your garden in the evening, after the heat of the day has passed, and less water will be lost to evaporation. The plants can then take a long, cool drink to build themselves up for another hot day.

Lawns obviously need water but in the early stages of a drought the best advice is to give the available water to your border plants and shrubs.

When you do come to water your lawn, give it a really good soak. This will ensure that the roots are drawn downwards rather than towards the surface. In a drought, let the grass grow to at least 2.5cm/1in long. It will endure the dry conditions much better and can be close mown later on.

Some spots in the garden are inevitably drier than others. Steps or paved areas are usually very free draining and so a broom like the Genista pilosa (top) makes an ideal choice.

Not all plants which thrive on dry soil are shrubby. Honesty, Lunaria biennis (above) is a pretty herbaceous plant which prefers a shady part of the garden. Delicate white or purple flowers disguise the fact that it is particularly robust and can withstand dry conditions. The silvery seed pods make beautiful additions to flower arrangements.

Dry and Shady Corners

Nearly every garden has a dry and shady corner but it need not be a problem area. There are many plants that will grow well in such conditions.

In sunny, open situations most plants thrive and put on a colourful display. Somewhere in your garden, however, there is bound to be a dry, shady area, under a tree, perhaps, or hard by a north-facing wall, where stunning colour is difficult to achieve. There is no need to despair; many plants will thrive in dry shade and turn problem areas into attractive focal points.

Woodland carpet

A ground-hugging carpet of foliage transforms dry shade under trees into an attractive woodland setting. It also suppresses weeds, which seem to prosper in any conditions. Ivy, a true woodland sprite, comes into its own in dry shade.

Variegated ivies such as *Hedera helix* 'Goldchild' and 'Glacier' will make a dash for areas of dappled shade, while common ivy, with its glossy green leaves, provides romantic, old-fashioned cover. For a lighter green ground cover and curly leaves grow *H. helix* 'Manda's Crested'.

Periwinkles, with glossy, light green leaves and soft blue flowers, cover dry, shady ground very quickly. There are variegated forms of both *Vinca major* and *V. minor*, but like variegated ivy they can only tolerate light shade.

Shady perennials

Many perennial plants are at home in dry shade. In spring, epimediums provide dainty

Dry shady conditions suit plants which grow wild at the edges of woodland, such as foxgloves (above).

Neil Holmes

Harry Smith Collection

Ivies are lovers of woodland conditions, including dry shade, and will bring colour and texture to spots where few other things will grow. The leaves of Hedera helix 'Manda's Crested' (left) turn coppery as winter approaches.

Various forms of spurge (Euphorbia spp.) grow well under trees, whence their cup-shaped golden-yellow bracts glow enticingly during the spring (right).

Peter McHoy

RECOMMENDED VARIETIES

Ground cover
Hedera helix 'Goldchild' has golden variegation and 'Glacier' has creamy-white edged leaves.
Vinca minor and *Vinca major* have attractive glossy green leaves and pretty blue flowers.

Perennials
Stinking hellebore (*Helleborus foetidus*) has dark, deeply divided evergreen leaves, and green, bell-shaped flowers with maroon rims in spring.
Euphorbias offer good stem colour and masses of bright golden-greeny flower heads.
Geranium phaeum and *Geranium macrorrhizum* have mounded foliage and purple to magenta flowers in summer.
Lady's mantle (*Alchemilla mollis*) has furry leaves and yellow-green flowers.
Heuchera sanguinea 'Bressingham Hybrids' have reddish pink flowers, and need dappled shade.

Shrubs
Spotted laurel (*Aucuba japonica*) has evergreen spotted golden leaves. Females bear red berries in autumn.

Climbers
Climbing hydrangea (*Hydrangea petiolaris*) is deciduous, but has good foliage and pretty flower panicles.
Persian ivy (*Hedera colchica* 'Sulphur Heart') has large floppy leaves with good bright colouring.
Winter-flowering jasmine (*Jasminium nudiflorum*) has fragrant yellow flowers in spring.

Ferns
Cretan brake (*Pteris cretica*) has yellow-green, deeply divided fronds and grows to 45cm/18in. It needs winter protection.
Rusty back fern (*Ceterach officinarum*) has fronds with rounded lobes and is semi-evergreen. The scales on the lower surface of the fronds mature from silver to bronze. It grows to 15cm/6in and suits the front of a shady area.

Bulbs
English bluebell has nodding stems of tubular blue flowers in spring.
Lily-of-the-valley (*Convallaria majalis*) has pretty and fragrant flower bells carried on arching stems in spring.

white or yellow flowers, carried above mounds of heart-shaped foliage. The spring leaves of some epimediums boast splendid bronze tones. Put these low-growing charmers at the front of a woodland planting under trees.

Stinking hellebore (*Helleborus foetidus*) enjoys a similar habitat. It carries its deeply divided dark green leaves all through the year, and in late winter to spring produces heads of small, bell-like, pale green flowers with a maroon rim. They grow to 45cm/18in, with a similar spread.

Wild wood flowers

Euphorbias are also useful under trees. Wood spurge (*Euphorbia amygdaloides*), in its form *rubra*, offers bright red stems, dark, evergreen foliage and the brightness of massed yellow-green flowerheads in spring. Plants grow to a height and spread of 30cm/1ft. Also suitable is *E. amygdaloides robbiae*, a shorter plant with looser flowerheads of light green bracts.

Foxgloves (*Digitalis* spp.) give a natural-looking woodland effect under trees. They self-seed abundantly, and carry colourful flowers on lofty, long-lasting spikes.

Various cranesbills (*Geranium* spp.) make good ground-

covering growth and produce pastel-coloured flowers. *G. macrorrhizum* has light green foliage and magenta summer flowers. Mourning widow (*G. phaeum*) carries its dark purple summer flowers above a light green foliage.

Lady's mantle (*Alchemilla mollis*) provides soft, furry foliage mounds and dainty yellow flowers in summer, while equally delicate flowers, in shades of red and pink, are of-

Photos Horticultural

DRY START

Under deciduous trees, plant ground cover in autumn when the leaves have fallen. The ground cover plants will have a good start in relatively warm, moist soil with good light.

By the time the leaves are out again in spring the ground cover will be well established.

Andrew Lawson

Good sources of floral colour in dry shady conditions include the magenta blooms of the delightfully dainty Geranium macrorrhizum (above), here pictured with Solomon's seal (Polygonatum), and the fresh greens of the stinking hellebore (Helleborus foetidus, left).

fered by heuchera (*Heuchera* 'Bressingham Hybrids'). Plant them at the outer edge of the tree canopy, as they are best in dappled or partial shade.

Shrubby shade-lovers

Various forms of spotted laurel (*Aucuba japonica*) provide glossy evergreen leaves in plain green or with golden variegations. If both male and female plants are planted, the females will bear bright red berries in autumn.

In the dry shade of walls or buildings, where indirect light is not restricted, variegated or

PLANTING UP A SHADY AREA

Use periwinkle and variegated ivy as the basic ground cover plants, with three or four plants for every square metre.

At random, in the middle of the planting area, set stinking hellebore, lady's mantle and mourning widow. Their foliage will rise above the ground cover and they will give a succession of flowers from early spring through to summer.

Towards the front, plant bulbs and lungwort (*Pulmonaria saccharata*) with its spotty evergreen leaves and pretty spring flowers. Combined, they provide early spring colour.

For autumn colour, plant white and pink flowered Japanese anemone (*Anemone japonica*). This tall-growing perennial carries its pastel flowers high on thin stems.

MULCH MAGIC

When you plant into a dry and shady bed at the foot of a north-facing wall, water the plants in well. Then add a thick layer of chipped bark, leaf mould or compost all round the plants. The mulch holds the water in the ground longer and stops excess water evaporation.

evergreen hollies make a bold splash of foliage colour.

On a shady wall or at the foot of a tall tree, plant the climbing hydrangea (*Hydrangea petiolaris*). Although it is deciduous, its spring and summer foliage and flowers make an attractive display.

Upwardly mobile

Ivies, too, can be used for upward cover in dry shade. For large, floppy, variegated leaves grow Persian ivy (*Hedera colchica* 'Sulphur Heart').

Winter-flowering jasmine (*Jasminum nudiflorum*) bears bright yellow flowers on leafless stems in the winter, and dark green leaves through the summer. It will need support.

Ferns

Many ferns will grow well in dry and shady situation, providing attractive shapes and delicate foliage.

Cretan brake (*Pteris cretica*), rusty-back fern (*Ceterach officinarum*) and fishtail fern

ACID TEST

If the soil in a dry, shady area is acid, you can grow rhododendrons and camellias for their evergreen foliage and strongly coloured spring flowers.

Pieris japonica 'Variegata', with its creamy-green foliage and pretty spring shoots and flowers, also grows well in these conditions.

Tania Midgley

Despite the restricted choice of plants, simple planting schemes can still grace a dry and shady spot (above). Here, a bed of bluebells dominates the scene, with Solomon's seal providing height at the back; the latter's greenish-white flowers emerge just after the bluebells have passed their best.

The evergreen leaves produced by heucheras make good ground cover, but they are usually grown for their summer flowers. Those of H. 'Red Spangles' (left above) are particularly colourful.

Most ferns enjoy wet conditions, but some can cope with a drier site. Among the best are Pteris cretica *'Major' (left), with its pale green wavy fronds, and* Ceterach officinarum, *with leathery, dark green, lobed foliage (below).*

FOOD AND DRINK

GARDEN NOTES

Before planting up the dry shady area prepare the ground so that the plants have the best start in life possible.

In autumn, dig the soil over and remove perennial weeds. Ground cover suppresses annual weeds but the perennial thugs need to be dug out.

Add bulky organic material to the soil and plant up the first layer of ground cover plants.

As you plant the areas up, water in well and mulch if possible. Keep plants well-watered during their first growing season, and in the case of shrubs, for the second growing season as well.

Once the plants are well-established, even though the conditions may not seem favourable, these specially chosen dry shade lovers will grow well.

Morley Read/Garden Picture Library

DRY AND SHADY CORNERS

ELEGANCE IN THE SHADE

BRIGHT IDEAS

Grow the elegant shrub *Garrya elliptica* with its glossy evergreen leaves and greyish-green, long tassel-like flowers. It provides subtle winter textures and combines well with the winter-flowering jasmine.

(*Cyrtomium falctatum*) offer interesting foliage in varying shades of green.

For a completely different effect, grow *Phyllitis scolopendrium* 'Crispum' with its upright, ribbon-like leaves. Common polypody (*Polypodium vulgare*) suits a shady area in a rock garden.

Bulbs

Many spring and autumn bulbs will provide generous displays that brighten up the dullest corners of the garden.

A traditional woodland favourite is the spring-flowering English bluebell. Its arching stems of soft blue, tubular flowers make a breath-taking display when massed in large clumps. Also useful is the shorter-growing Spanish bluebell or scilla.

Spring flowering lily-of-the-valley (*Convallaria majalis*) and Solomon's seal (*Polygonatum* spp.) will produce delicate flowers in poor conditions.

Hardy autumn and winter-flowering cyclamens do well in dry shade but need shelter from cold winds. Their marbled leaves will provide interest for much of the year.

Shady retreat

Include a seat of wood or iron so you can enjoy your shady glade as a quiet retreat from the brighter, more showy parts of the garden.

Planting up the shady area will be challenging, but the resulting combination of foliage colour and texture with subtle flowers will make a tranquil haven on hot days.

33

Light and Shade

Deep shade and harsh, unremitting sunlight can both cause problems in the garden; the solution lies in altering the conditions or finding the plants to suit them.

Many plants are at their best in sunny situations, while others prefer partial or dappled shade. Extremes of sunlight and of shade can create problems for plants and for gardeners alike.

A town garden that faces north and is surrounded by buildings and garden walls may occasionally be a welcome cool haven. Most of the time, though, it feels and is sunless and dull. In a larger, more open garden, there may still be dark and shady sites that you wish to lighten up.

Fortunately there are many practical ways to brighten and lighten a shady garden or to create shade and shelter in an exposed and sunny site.

Let there be light

If shade is caused by mature trees, the remedy is to thin out the crown. This is difficult and dangerous work and should only be carried out by qualified and properly insured professional tree surgeons.

If the trees are young and the branches accessible it is possible to raise or 'lift' the head of a tree by removing some of the lower branches.

You are entitled to cut back any tree branches overhanging your boundary fence or wall, though, in the interest of neighbourliness, it is best to tell your neighbour politely

Light and shade is an important element in gardening; it determines which plants will grow well in a particular site and which areas of the garden will be most suitable for sitting areas, ponds, or other features, as well as being a design element in its own right. Dappled shade (above) makes agreeable, ever-changing patterns as the sun moves through the sky.

34

Andrew Lawson

You can make the most of the available light in deeply shaded areas by painting walls white, or another light, reflective shade, and by using white furnishings (above).

The simplest solution to excessively bright or shady areas of the garden is to find plants to suit the environment. A sunny spot will accommodate a riotous display of colourful bulbs and annuals (right), while plants which grow naturally in woodland or woodland edge conditions, such as the foxgloves (below) suit shade. This delightful yellow species is Digitalis ambigua.

what you intend doing.

If the tree is in your garden, and you decide that removing it entirely is the only solution, you will definitely need expert help. It will also be necessary to discover from your local council if a preservation order applies to your tree.

Hedge shade

If hedge shrubs or trees, especially the fast-growing Leyland cypress, are left to grow tall, this defeats the object of the hedge, as there is a loss of lower dense foliage cover. The best solution is to cut back the hedge's top growth, though not too drastically. It may take several years to reduce a rampant hedge to the required height without damaging its top.

Shade caused by buildings and garden walls can be mitigated by painting the walls, creating more reflected light. White is the popular choice, but if you prefer a colour, keep to pale or pastel shades.

With higher light levels you will be able to grow a wider variety of plants, especially variegated foliage plants that need extra light to look their best. The reflected light will also make the garden a brighter and pleasanter place for you to relax in.

If the shady area is small and close to the house, you might consider lighting it. Then, when you sit outside on summer evenings it will be bright enough to enjoy. Keep unwanted insect guests at bay with insect-repelling amber or yellow light bulbs.

Mirror images

In a small town garden, mirrors fixed to courtyard and boundary walls give an illusion of space as well as reflecting available light.

Used without embellishment, a mirror makes a fairly bald statement, but it can be made to look natural by framing it with climbing plants. A ledge or shelf in front of the mirror makes a useful site for pots or containers with trailing or hanging plants.

Prepare the mirror for outdoor use by lining its back with aluminium foil. Mount and frame the back and edges of the mirror with treated wood and use mirror glass thicker than 5mm/$\frac{1}{5}$ in.

In a shady garden area, use white metal or plastic outdoor furniture to add to the light effects. White Versailles tubs in wood or plastic will reflect available light and add to the overall brighter look.

Use light or white coloured statuary or ornaments to make dramatic focal points in

Don Wildridge

Marijke Heuff/Garden Picture Library

WATER IN TIME

GROWING TIPS

Plants in dry shade under trees, hedges or in a rain shadow area at the base of a wall will need extra water in very hot conditions.

Keep a watering can on hand so that you can provide them with a weekly watering before they become parched.

WHICH SHADE?

In shady areas near streams or ponds the soil is usually very moist and may even be waterlogged at times.

Plants that enjoy these boggy conditions include marsh marigold (*Caltha palustris*), mimulus hybrids and astilbe. Various primula species such as giant cowslip (*P. florindae*) and japanese primrose (*P. japonica*) provide delicate flowers in spring and summer.

Woodland shade is damp, but not waterlogged and is enjoyed by many flowering plants including *Dicentra formosa* 'Pearl Drops'. Low-growing hardy cyclamens (*Cyclamen hederifolium*) brighten the shade in autumn, while the tall sprays of mauve flowers of *Thalictrum delavayi* provide colour in summer.

Many wild plants are natural woodland dwellers. Lesser celandine and yellow archangel (*Lamium galeobdolon*), for example, offer pretty yellow flowers and interesting foliage ground cover.

In dry shade under trees or near hedges, *Euphorbia amygdaloides* 'Rubra' puts on a spring display with bright reddish-maroon stems and yellowy-green bracts and flowers. *Heuchera sanguinea* 'Bressingham Hybrids' makes a pretty ground cover with its mounds of marbled leaves. The tiny flowers, carried on thin stems, seem to dance on the air.

Helleborus foetidus makes a pretty spring show with its pale green bell-like flowers held high above deeply cut evergreen foliage. Planted in massed numbers under trees it makes a very light ground cover.

Tania Midgley

shady areas. The deep shade of a laurel glade, for instance, can be lifted by the addition of accents such as a white bench or a striking piece of mock-classical statuary.

If the shaded area has an ordinary, well-drained, loam soil, there are many flowering and foliage plants you can grow to lift the gloom. Many aquilegias do well in shade, including *A. alpina* 'Hensol Harebell', which bears deep blue flowers in early summer.

Foxgloves enjoy woodland shade conditions, and will seed themselves abundantly for future flowers. A short form, growing to 90cm/3ft, *Digitalis ambigua* is a bold and bright choice with golden-yellow trumpets. In spring, the sunny flowers of a variety of spring daisy, *Doronicum plantagineum* 'Harpur Crewe', will bring shafts of golden light to shine in the shade.

White-flowered plants are very stylish and offer the simplest way to brighten up the

Photos Horticultural

Peter McHoy

area. *Phlox paniculata* 'Alba' and *Campanula latifolia* 'Alba' provide tall heads of white flowers in late or mid summer.

Variegated ivy will do well in dappled shade and will clamber up vertical surfaces towards the light. The glossy leaves of the variegated *Pachysandra terminalis* 'Variegata' offer good ground cover.

Covering up

If your garden is exposed to too much sunlight, there are several practical remedies. For quick results, building wooden trellis and screen block walling is the best choice.

For permanent overhead shading, install a pergola clad with attractive climbing plants. For a not-so-permanent effect, a large rectangular umbrella will provide a stylish, holiday atmosphere on a sun-drenched patio. In winter store it indoors or in a garden shed. Then you will have maximum winter light and a shaded area in summer.

Screening trellis work, open

Plants with strong, sculptural shapes such as New Zealand flax (Phormium tenax) can make good use of open, sunny sites, where they will cast strong shadows. The variety 'Purpureum' (above left) adds to its appeal with good leaf colour.

An alternative way of providing interest in a dark corner is with a piece of statuary or other stone feature (left).

The dry shade of a large tree makes planting difficult, but the addition of a bench or other seating makes a cool haven from which to enjoy the sunnier parts of the garden (above).

Shady woodland conditions suit Campanula latifolia, whose delicate white bells shine softly through the late summer (right).

Tania Midgely

Sites near to the house are often either too dark or too bright. Those on the shady side are best planted with a display of foliage plants (left), while sunnier situations suit colourful annuals and herbs, protected from the drying sun by a seasonal screen created by growing a deciduous climber on an open trellis (right).

Wood spurge (Euphorbia amygdaloides) is a shade-loving plant with sunny flowers made up of yellow bracts. 'Rubra', also known as 'Purpurea' (below) adds reddish-purple stems to its considerable charms.

A north-facing wall at the end of a narrow garden presents planting problems. One solution is to plant fragrant climbers to find the light and to create a kind of minimal arbour with a seat that looks back along the garden (below right). If the seating is painted white, as here, so much the better.

block walls and pergolas can all be used to support plants, which will soften the look of their supports. Although you are aiming to create shade, use plants that provide delicate screening or are deciduous, so that you have high light levels in winter. Climbing roses, wisteria and many varieties of clematis offer good seasonal shading.

Shadow play

Trees such as birch are suitable as seasonal screens. In summer, their delicate leaves and thin branches make a dappled shade. In winter, when the leaves have fallen, the framework of branches and twigs makes an interesting tracery effect against the sky, and allows all the available light to filter through.

On a patio or in a garden where there is strong and in-

Peter McHoy

A TRICK OF THE LIGHT

If you have a long narrow garden you can make two types of garden by some creative deception. Near the house plant trees and shrubs closely so that it appears that you have a small garden. All that will be visible from the house is a densely planted, shady area.

Make the rest of the garden open and lighter-looking; keep the plantings in this part of the garden near the edges and going up walls.

Using this device you will have the chance to use both plants that thrive in shade and those that prefer a more open aspect to create two separate gardens with very different atmospheres.

S & O Mathews

tense sunlight, use plants to make large and emphatic shadows. A large terracotta tub planted with an striking, architectural plant such as New Zealand flax (*Phormium tenax*), will make a strong statement. Place it so that its huge shadow can be cast onto a white wall or spread dramatically across a close-cut lawn.

An unadorned pergola will look effective if its strong parallel lines can be picked up as shadows on a wall. You can also cheat a little bit by painting darker areas onto a wall and pretending they are the shadows of the overhead pergola. It will create a talking point, and may make you feel the area is more shaded than it actually is.

At night, carefully planned lighting concealed behind dramatic plants will make interesting and effective shadow play. If your patio is used at night as an extended dining area, the lighting will provide you with a sense of extra space and add a theatrical effect to outdoor entertaining.

In the Shade

If you have a corner that doesn't see the light, there is a wide range of shade-loving plants to bring it beautifully to life.

Think of the shade in your garden as an advantage! Many plants thrive in cool places and are under less stress from water loss. Early spring-flowering bulbs are at their best in shade, and camellias prefer shade because early morning winter sun can damage their leaves and petals.

Woodland plants grow best under the cover of trees. For a pretty show of spring flowers, primroses, bergenia, hellebore, Solomon's seal, bleeding heart, pulmonaria and periwinkle all do well in shade.

Well contained

You can grow fairly large shrubs and even small trees in containers in the shade. Bulbs and spring and summer bedding plants also perform well in such conditions. There are, however, several key factors for successful plants in a contained environment. You will have to provide them with the right growing medium, adequate water, fertilizer and, if necessary, winter protection. Choose your plants according to the size of container and your own seasonal favourites.

Being choosy

Although you can grow many of these plants from seed, it will take some time before they are large enough to make an impression in a container. It is therefore better to buy young plants from garden centres or nurseries.

Choose your container for the look you want to create, considering the number of plants and their ultimate size. In a garden setting or patio,

stone urns, terracotta pots, sinks, old baths and iron water tanks can all be used for a variety of effects. On a balcony, where stone containers may be too heavy when filled, you may like to consider lightweight plastic replica versions.

This imposing terracotta tub gives a sunny display even though it is in the shade. There are a wide range of leaf colours and shapes to add interest and the yellow tobacco plant is night scented too.

When you begin to prepare the container for planting, place it in position before you fill it with soil and plants. You can then see what it looks like before it becomes too heavy.

Make sure that your container has drainage holes in

the base. Before you add soil, make a good drainage layer. Place a layer of crocks in the bottom of the container, then cover this layer with clean gravel. Water the containers regularly – preferably every day – when they are planted up, particularly during prolonged hot, dry weather.

Good drainage

Containers planted under trees should be lined with plastic before planting so that a reservoir of water is held in the base. Plant up as normal, with a layer of drainage material. The water will then drain away from the roots and prevent them rotting, but is stored so that it is available when the plants need it.

To promote good growth, use a soil-based compost and mix in fertilizer before you plant the container. In spring, loosen the surface of the container,

Herald the spring in even the dullest of corners by planting up lots of pots with bulbs. Instead of mixing plants stick to one type and colour in each one. Simple terracotta pots (right) are transformed by dazzling white hyacinths and vibrant yellow daffodils.

Creating a look that is completely different, this white chair (below) makes an unusual pedestal for a plant display – and helps drainage. Trailing ivy softens the edges of an elegant grecian style trough. The overgrown trellis creates a shaded environment which is used here to best advantage.

Photos Horticultural

Tommy Candler/Garden Picture Library

if it is a large one, and add a top-dressing of new compost. For plants that prefer acid soils use a proprietary lime-free or ericaceous compost which contains the correct balance of nutrients.

Colour planning

For the brightest burst of early colour some of the most rewarding container-grown plants are spring-flowering bulbs. Prepare your containers in the autumn; you could, for instance, plant up small terracotta pots with tulips. Plant two or three winter-flowering pansies in each pot. The pansies will supply colour through the winter and in spring the bulbs will flower through the pansy mounds.

Although one large shrub can look very effective in a pot, why not surround it with flowers to give a new effect with each season? Plant small bulbs, like allium or snake's head fritillary (*Fritillaria meleagris*) around the edge and leave them undisturbed. When they have finished flowering

they will only look untidy for a few weeks until their foliage dies back. In the centre of the container plant a permanent shrub such as camellia. In spring sow trailing lobelia seeds around the shrub. In summer they will tumble over

the edge of the pot and make a colourful groundcover. Camellias like a lime-free or acid soil, so top-dress them after flowering with an ericaceous compost.

The dramatic strap-like

SHADY SHRUBS	FLOWERS AND FOLIAGE
Japanese azaleas	Evergreen; many flower colours. Acid lover
Camellia japonica and × *williamsia* varieties	Evergreen; many flower colours. Acid lover
Skimmia japonica	Evergreen; needs male and female plants
Mahonia aquifolium	Evergreen; yellow flowers, purple berries
floribunda roses	Many flowers
Pieris formosa	Evergreen; red leaves in spring; white flowers. Acid lover
CLIMBERS AND WALL SHRUBS	**FLOWERS AND FOLIAGE**
flowering quince	Spring flowers
Hydrangea petiolaris	White lace-cap flowers
'*Zephirine Drouhin' rose	Perfumed. Dead head for long flowering
*winter-flowering jasmine	Delicate yellow flowers on bare stems
*summer-flowering jasmine	White perfumed flowers, feathery leaves
Clematis alpina	Spring flowers
Clematis 'Nelly Moser'	Large pink flowers
Clematis macropetala	Bell-shaped blue flowers
ivies	Evergreen; wide range of leaf colours and shapes.
holly	Evergreen; variegated or plain leaves. Berries
firethorn	Evergreen; clusters of small flowers. Bright berries
cotoneaster	Evergreen; tiny flowers, berries

* These climbers need the support of trellis, stakes or wires

Tania Midgley

If you have only enough room for one container plant then this evergreen Pieris formosa 'Forrestii' (above) is an excellent choice. Its young leaves are brilliant red and it produces clusters of white flowers in the spring so there is always something new to look out for.

These colourful flowers (below) seem to cascade down the steps. With a pot positioned on each step the plants mingle and hide the containers.

leaves of New Zealand flax (*phormium tenax*), offers a striking fan-shaped outline and good colour all year round. There are many different coloured forms including some with purple to bronze foliage, others are striped yellow and green. Protect it in hard winters by spreading a straw mulch around its feet and wrap it with hessian sacking.

Climbing plants

Many climbing plants do well in containers in shady corners. They will not be as rampant as they might in a sunnier position, but they offer colourful cover for walls. Climbers can also be coaxed up trees.

The climbing hydrangea,

Hydrangea petiolaris, likes shade but is a slow starter. Once it gets going, however, it provides a show of pretty lace-cap flowers and glossy green leaves.

Shady scents

Some climbing roses, too, do just as well in shade as in sun. Perfume, lovely flowers and pretty foliage in spring are their gifts to the garden. Flowering from spring until autumn, the thornless rose, 'Zephirine Drouhin', is unbeatable. Make sure that it is well supported by canes in the container and remove all faded flower heads promptly to keep a succession of flowers going.

For a complete summer and

Ann Kelly/Garden Picture Library

winter picture plant a large container with the dainty, yellow-flowered winter jasmine, *Jasminum nudiflorum*, and the white-flowered summer jasmine, *Jasminum officinale*. They both perform well in shade, have delicate foliage and pretty fragrance.

Clematis is a favourite garden plant and many do grow well in containers in the shade. They all like a cool root run and plenty of moisture. *C. macropetala* flowers later in spring making a pretty cover as it tumbles over the edges of the container. Of the large-flowered clematis varieties 'Nelly Moser' is best as it keeps its colour better in shade.

Evergreen favourites

Evergreens are a great advantage in shady situations. They do not always have green foliage: some have mixed white and green colourings or variegations and some have attractive buttery golden markings.

Bear in mind, however, that in dense shade they may not be as bright as they would be in a sunnier situation. Many evergreens have brightly coloured berries in autumn, lasting through the winter.

Holly, firethorn and cotoneaster suit container growth in shady corners. Ivy can be used to brighten and soften shady

PROJECT PLANTING UP POTS

Select the position for the container before adding soil. Make sure the tub has drainage holes in the base. Place a layer of crocks in the bottom and cover with a layer of gravel. Use a soil-based compost and mix in a little fertilizer before you plant. Arrange the plants then firm into position. Water well.

Harry Smith

spots and comes in a wide range of leaf colours and shapes. Depending on which ivy you choose you can use it to tumble over containers or climb up walls, trellis and trees. *Hedera colchica* 'Sulphur Heart' (sometimes sold as 'Paddy's Pride') has a yellow splash of colour in the centre of its leaves. Give it a cane or trellis support when you plant it in a container under a tree

Delicate flowers may survive in shady corners as shade and shelter often go hand in hand. An exquisite selection of plants (below) in fragile, subtle colours makes a permanent floral arrangement. Silvery trailing Helichrysum petiolatum, petunias, lobelia and daisy-like chrysanthemums look wonderful together.

SHADY SPOTS

● A shady stairway down to a basement flat is an ideal situation for a series of pots. Create a mass of colour or select just one.
● If you have an old tree in a shady spot, cloak it in clematis.
● On a shady windowsill, plant up a window box with bright violas and ivies, for long-lasting colour and interest. In the winter, use winter-flowering varieties of viola.

BRIGHT IDEAS

and it will soon climb strongly. For a reddish-purple colour in winter use *Hedera helix* 'Atropurpurea'. Its dark leaves turn a bronze to purple colour in winter.

Foliage and flowers

Many shrubs have such lovely foliage that their flowers almost pale into insignificance. The spotted laurel, *Aucuba*

japonica, has glossy green leaves and bright red berries in autumn. *A.j.* 'Maculata' has bright, yellow-splashed leaves. The flowers, small, green and star-shaped, appear in spring. For a bolder colour effect, underplant the container with daffodil bulbs in autumn. In spring they will make a stunning display against the glossy leaves and star shaped flowers of the aucuba.

Floribunda roses look good in containers on a patio or balcony. They need to have a good deal of space for their roots, so make sure the container you use is at least 38cm/15in deep. Dwarf floribundas, too, can be used for a colourful display in a container. Provide good drainage and never let the container get water-logged. Feed roses twice a year, when spring growth is beginning and again in mid-summer. In return they will provide a bright spot for a shady corner.

EWA

Planting Under Trees

Make the most of any ornamental or specimen tree by surrounding its base with a changing, seasonal carpet of colourful plants.

Photos Horticultural

By underplanting a tree with shrubs, ground cover or carpeting plants and perhaps a few bulbs, it can be made to blend harmoniously into its surroundings. Not only is the result more interesting, it also makes better use of valuable space – and cuts down on tedious weeding!

The best trees for underplanting are ornamental species that cast light shade. Small to medium-sized varieties with pretty foliage or dramatic shapes are particularly suitable. Many medium-sized ornamental conifers are also ideal for underplanting – especially architecturally shaped or colourful varieties.

If you have large mature trees that cast very heavy shade, do not try growing the

Andrew Lawson

44

TREES TO UNDERPLANT

The following trees cast only light shade.
Ballerina apple trees
Weeping birch *Betula pendula*)
Flaking bark birches (eg *Betula utilis, B. papyrifera* etc)
Crab apples (eg *Malus* 'John Downie' with large, red, edible fruit, *M.* 'Golden Hornet' with round yellow fruit)
Ornamental cherries (eg *Prunus* 'Amanogawa' with upright stems, *P.* 'Cheal's Weeping')
Conifers (eg silver spruce, golden Irish yew, *Cedrus deodara* 'Pendula') *Gleditsia triacanthos* 'Sunburst'
Maples (eg *Acer negundo* 'Flamingo', Japanese maples).

sort of ornamental under-planting discussed here. Instead, choose plants that thrive in dry, shady conditions (see 'Dry and Shady Corners' in *My Garden* part 37).

The options

The idea of underplanting is to create a continuous carpet of plants under something taller. The 'carpet' can take different forms and be of various heights and colours.

You could use a spectacular mixture of different plant types to give a tall underplanting, reminiscent of a miniature mixed border. You could go for lower-growing ground cover plants – lower still – dwarf carpeting plants.

Bulbs are useful for introducing colour that changes

In midsummer, hosta's decorative flower spikes rise gracefully above its foliage (left), adding height and colour to the underplanting of an Acer japonicum 'Aureum'.

An attractive planting scheme is the conifer, Cedrus deodara (above), underplanted with pinks (Dianthus spp). More extensive ground cover for conifers and heathers can be provided by Anemone blanda (right).

For an all-green scheme, plant Pachysandra terminalis (below) to provide carpeting ground cover.

PLANTING SCHEMES FOR DIFFERENT TREES

Weeping birch
Dwarf rhododendron, camellia or pieris; carpet of heathers (choose different species to flower throughout the year).

Weeping deodara (*Cedrus deodara* 'Pendula')
Ornamental grasses such as *Stipa gigantea* (which has oat-like heads over leaves like pampas grass); carpet of mixed geranium species.

Blue spruce (*Picea pungens* 'Hoopsii or 'Hoto')
Carpet of *Anemone blanda* in mixed colours with groups of Himalayan blue poppies (*Meconopsis betonicifolia*) and white Japanese anemones.

Crab apple or flowering cherry
Mixture of old-fashioned cottage garden flowers like bergenia, perennial forget-me-not (*Brunnera macrophylla*), *Geranium phaeum lividum* (which has lilac flowers in mid summer) and herbaceous penstemon, which flowers in late summer through to autumn.

Conifer
Bamboo or one of the miscanthus (ornamental sugar cane) varieties, or a mixture of striking grasses, such as gardener's garters (*Phalaris arundinacea* 'Picta'), *Helichtotrichon sempervirens* (blue) and *Deschampsia caespitosa* 'Bronze Veil' (bronze).

Medium Conifer
Epimedium × *rubrum* (red flowers, semi-evergreen leaves); *Imperata cylindrica rubra* (blood red grass).

Maples (*Acer* spp)
Carpet of hostas, Solomon's seal, lady's mantle, dog's tooth violets and *Viola labradorica*.

Snowy mespilus (*Amelanchier* spp)
Carpet of autumn crocus (*Crocus speciosus*) and spring tulips.

Gleditsia triacanthos 'Sunburst'
Carpet of purple sage (*Salvia officinalis* 'Purpurascens').

Ballerina apple tree
Rose 'The Fairy' (60-90cm/2-3ft high, pink flowers); group of *Gypsophila paniculata* 'Bristol Fairy' or a carpet of *Stachys lanata*.

Photos Horticultural

dramatically over the season – especially with evergreen trees that change little.

The possibilities are endless. If you have several trees, try different ideas, perhaps on seasonal themes, and see how they bring the garden to life!

Tall underplanting

You can underplant a tree with relatively tall shrubs, like roses or herbaceous flowers, creating the same effect as with a small ornamental tree planted at the back of a large mixed border. Pick some border plants, and design a small group to go under a tree.

Choose a mixture of contrasting shapes and tall and

Tania Midgley

46

short plants to put under a tree for the most interesting results (see box). This sort of mixed group looks good planted in grass as a feature, perhaps in a front garden.

Ground cover

Low shrubby plants under a tree can be a very effective easy-care grouping.

Try an evergreen like Mexican orange (*Choisya ternata*) or a conifer underplanted with prostrate cotoneasters. This may seem an obvious choice but it is not difficult to dream up exciting new combinations.

Try teaming trees that provide spring flowers and late summer fruits with a 30-45cm/ 12-18in deep carpet of mixed herbaceous or old fashioned flowers. Or grow conifers with colourful perennial grasses and creeping cranesbills for a strikingly different look.

Carpeting

Carpets of dwarf bulbs such *Anemone blanda*, hardy cyclamen and autumn-flowering *Crocus speciosus* look good under most trees. Keep the cost down by planting thinly and waiting a few years for them to spread naturally; leave the dead flower-heads so they self seed.

Alternatively, choose low creeping plants such as Irish ivy (*Hedera hibernica*), which is a good carpeter. You could add *Pachysandra terminalis* (there is a very pretty variegated version which looks good under all-green trees) and the acid-loving *Gaultheria procumbens* (a dwarf evergreen with red berries in autumn) which are both very pretty.

If you have a lightly canopied sub-tropical tree, why not surround it with formal summer bedding, followed by bulbs and/or wallflowers for spring.

Wild or woodland

In a woodland garden, underplanting trees is essential. Plant well-defined patches of

Spring bulbs such as tulips and grape hyacinths (left) are classic under-tree plantings. Here, they wonderfully enhance the soft pink blooms of the flowering cherry, Prunus 'Cheal's Weeping'.

Clever underplanting of a mature apple tree with tulips, honesty and euphorbia (above) give this garden corner a charming, natural look.

The bright, cheerful colours (below left) of wallflower, which blooms in spring and early summer, are pleasantly softened by the dappled sunlight through the tree above.

The dense, silvery leaves and tiny pink summer flowers of Lamium 'Beacon Silver' (right) make interesting ground cover beneath the bronze-leaved Japanese maple, Acer palmatum 'Inabashidare'.

S & O Mathews

Photos Horticultural

- Choose ornamental trees that cast light shade for ornamental underplanting.
- If you have large mature trees that cast heavy shade, choose highly shade-tolerant plants that thrive in dry soil.
- Prepare soil well before underplanting. Do not dig deeply, as tree roots will be close to the surface. Instead, loosen soil with the points of a fork and work in some organic matter and Growmore or blood, fish and bone 120g per square metre/4oz per square yard. After planting, add a 5-8cm/2-3in layer of organic mulch.

Trees take up lots of nutrients from the soil, so feed plants under them every 6-8 weeks from early spring to late summer. Use Growmore or blood, fish and bone at 60g per square metre/2oz per square yard if soil is moist. If it is dry use a diluted liquid feed. Top up mulch with 2.5cm/1in of organic material every spring.

- After about two years, plants should cover the ground and very little weeding will be needed. Until then, weed frequently to prevent small plants being smothered. To avoid weeding altogether, cover the ground with black polythene before underplanting. Cut holes and plant through these, then cover the plastic with gravel or chipped bark.

Photos Horticultural

mixed, shade-tolerant wild flowers in long grass. Or grow single species carpets of blue-bells, wild daffodils, wood anemones or celandines.

These can be surrounded by closer mown areas of grass. Or you can edge your underplanting with logs and have a rustic path of wood chippings wind-

ing between the trees.

Fruit trees can be underplanted, provided they are well established and growing on fairly vigorous rootstocks that do not mind competition.

Since most fruit trees produce quite heavy shade, it is important to choose plants that are shade tolerant. Wild strawberries and buckler-leaved sorrel are two of the best edible carpeting plants for shade.

Ballerina apple trees give so little shade, you could grow most low fruit beneath them. Try strawberries, gooseberries and red currants, or even low-growing vegetables such as dwarf French beans, dwarf peas, lettuce and herbs.

Seasonal effects

For the most dramatic effect, the tree and its underplanting should be at their best at the

S & O Mathews

Tulips and daffodils (left) reach up to meet the hanging branches of Young's weeping birch (Betula pendula 'Youngii'), a lovely specimen tree for a smallish garden.

Begonia semperflorens (right) is an excellent underplanter, providing bright, tiny flowers in summer.

What could be more enchanting in autumn than this corner (below right) where Cyclamen africanum *and autumn crocuses (*Colchicum autumnale*), nudged by a late flowering hydrangea, hug the base of a mature tree trunk.*

In late spring, a subtly-coloured and fragrant spot can be created (below) with the delightful pendant blooms of the bird cherry tree (Prunus padus), happily teamed with the delicate blossoms of lilacs.

Don Wildridge

same time.

For spring, team a flowering tree, like an ornamental cherry, with a carpet of spring-flowering bulbs such as tulips. For an autumn display, choose a tree with good autumn colour, like many of the acers, underplanted with a ground covering shrub with good berries, such as *Gaultheria procumbens*, or with autumn crocus or colchicums, or perhaps an autumn-flowering cyclamen.

Alternatively, if your garden has seasonal 'gaps' when nothing much is looking its best, design your underplanting to bring a bright carpet of colour into the scheme at just the right times.

Harry Smith Collection

Ground-cover Plants

Bare patches of soil in the garden are an open invitation for weeds. Ground cover in borders, beds and on slopes can help to eliminate this problem and cut down on weeding, one of the gardener's most tedious chores.

Pat Brindley

Bugle (Ajuga reptans) is a hardy, evergreen perennial (left) which flowers in spring but provides year-round cover. The plant shown here is 'Variegata'. Other well-known varieties are 'Atropurpurea', which has dark bronze-purple leaves and 'Multicolor' (also known as 'Rainbow') which has tri-coloured leaves.

Photos Horticultural

When gardeners refer to ground cover, what they are really talking about is a permanent planting over every bare patch of soil, so weeds have no chance to grow.

Weed seeds, like all seeds, need light to germinate; if no light can reach the surface of the soil, you automatically control further weed growth. Similarly, seed that blows in or is dropped by birds has to land on bare soil in order to germinate. If you can reduce the area of bare ground in the garden, you reduce the weed problem too.

You may think that a lawn is ground cover, but it fails the other test of true ground cover – that of low maintenance once it is established. Your aim should be to plant up an area which will later need little or no further work.

Ground cover can be used anywhere, but it is most useful for areas of bare soil that you find difficult or time consuming to keep weed free.

Plants are far more attractive than bare ground anyway, so it is really only your budget which prevents you from covering every square inch of ground with plants.

Once you have bought a few plants, however, you can easily multiply them by dividing the crowns (if they are herbaceous perennials), or by taking cuttings or removing trailing stems which root down as they grow. Plant out the new plants so that they will eventually form a carpet.

The hallmark of ground cover is a spread of the same type of plant, providing a backcloth of greenery, with perhaps a splash of colour at flowering or berry time. For extra impact, you can plant individual shrubs, bulbs or other plants that contrast well with it.

Areas to cover

Ground cover brings lushness to the bare areas of your garden. Do you need it between established trees and shrubs?

For a thick carpet of semi-evergreen ground cover try one of the barrenworts such as Epimedium perralderianum (below right). It is a perennial which grows to a height of 30cm/12in and has yellow flowers in spring.

If you want ground cover that provides rich late summer and autumn colour the ice-plant (Sedum spectabile) is a good choice. The variety here (below) is 'Autumn Joy'. The variety 'Brilliant' has lighter rose-pink flowers. These members of the stonecrop family are fully hardy perennials that form clumps 45cm/18in wide and grow to a similar height. They look very good, as here, surrounding the base of trees.

SLOPES

An area which slopes lends itself to trailing plants – place them at the top of the slope and let gravity and nature do the rest. Clematis looks superb over a large area – they can grow to 10m/30ft or more. Choose the species rather than hybrids, which need pruning. Aubrietas, *Alyssum saxatile*, arabis and cerastium also spread over slopes to colourful effect.

Peter McHoy

Peter McHoy

On steep slopes where routine access is daunting? In shade where you cannot think of plants to grow? At the base of climbing plants? In tubs and troughs? Or in awkward areas between buildings and below fences, where weeds grow and seed into the rest of the garden? All are potential places to grow ground cover.

The choice of plants

Many plants are suitable for ground cover but there are some pointers to bear in mind. The plants must be perennial so that the cover is maintained from year to year. Evergreen plants are preferable, because they cover the soil all year round. However, many that die back in winter (herbaceous) or lose leaves from woody stems (deciduous) still prevent weeds from establishing, because their roots make a dense mat just below the surface, forming a hard, dry barrier against weeds.

Plants which spread quickly or are easy to propagate are ideal for covering large areas. Bear in mind, though, that those which spread by underground growth can pop up on the wrong side of paths and fences and become a nuisance.

Those that spread above ground can be sheared when they reach the edge of the area you want them to fill. Some plants do not know when to stop; rose of Sharon (*Hypericum calycinum*) and strawberries, for instance, can be a real nuisance.

Plants which spread outwards rather than upwards are good for covering areas quickly. Plants which trail, such as ivy or clematis, are just as happy sprawling over the ground as climbing up a support. Spreading plants

Peter McHoy

The dappled leaves of this lungwort (Pulmonaria species) provide a delightful contrast of light and shade (left). The different species of lungwort can have red, white or blue flowers. Most bloom in spring. They are hardy perennials which prefer shade. Pulmonaria is particularly useful as ground cover in the front of a border.

GROUND COVER PLANTS FOR SUN

Anthemis nobilis (camomile)

Arabis albida

Aubrieta deltoidea

Alyssum saxatile

Ceanothus thyrsiflorus repens

Centaurea 'John Coutts'

Cerastium tomentosum (snow-in-summer)

Ceratostigma plumbaginoides (shrubby plumbago)

Cistus parviflorus (rock rose)

Cytisus × kewensis (broom)

Daboecia cantabrica (Irish heath)

Dianthus hybrids (pinks)

Erica carnea (winter-flowering heather)

Genista lydia (broom)

Hebe albicans

Helianthemum hybrids (rock rose)

Iberis sempervirens 'Snowflake' (perennial candytuft)

Polygonum affine 'Superbum'

Polygonum vacciniifolium

Potentilla davurica 'Manchu'

Potentilla 'Elizabeth'

Sedum spathulifolium (stonecrop)

Sedum spurium (stonecrop)

Thymus serpyllum (thyme)

need not be low-growing, and can in fact be several feet high. They are still good ground cover providing that, like conifers for example, they form a fairly dense cover.

Points to watch

Some plants need attention to keep them looking good and are not suitable for areas with difficult access. Heathers, for instance, should be sheared back after flowering to keep the cover dense and low. Rose of Sharon also needs shearing to rejuvenate it after a hard winter and this can be a time-consuming job.

You should also be wary of plants which tend to die back from the centre. These need to be dug up, divided and replanted after discarding the dead sections. This is not much of a chore for one or two plants, but a whole carpet of them means a lot of work and loss of ground cover while they knit together again. Camomile, hebe and mossy saxifrages all have this tendency.

Matching your style

If you have an informal style of garden, as long as you consider the soil and the amount of shade the plant will tolerate, you can choose any type of cover. You may want a plant which will spread to all

Photos Horticultural

The true geraniums (above) are ideal for underplanting in a bed below shrubs. The variety shown is Geranium × cantabrigiense. Most geraniums prefer sun but some do better in shade. When selecting plants from the wide variety of geraniums available at garden centres, do bear in mind that some are only half hardy.

GARDEN NOTES

MOIST SHADE

Sites shaded by buildings or fences are usually moist and these are easily planted up with any of the plants recommended for shade (see chart). Remember, though, that the soil within about 60cm/2ft of a wall or fence will be very dry.

Harry Smith Collection

GROUND COVER PLANTS FOR SHADE

Ajuga reptans (bugle)

Alchemilla mollis (ladies' mantle)

Asarum europaeum (wild ginger)

Asperula odorata (sweet woodruff)

Bergenia species (elephant's ears)

Blechnum spicant (hard fern)

Clematis orientalis

Cornus canadensis

Cotoneaster conspicuus

Cotoneaster dammeri

Cotoneaster 'Gnome'

Cotoneaster microphyllus

Dicentra formosa (bleeding heart)

Epimedium species (barrenwort)

Euonymus fortunei radicans

Euphorbia robbiae

Gaultheria procumbens

Geranium species (not hybrids)

Geum × borisii

Hedera species (ivy)

Hosta species

Juniperus × media 'Pfitzeriana'

Lamium maculatum

Mahonia aquifolium

Pachysandra terminalis

Prunus laurocerasus 'Otto Luyken'

Pulmonaria species (lungwort)

Symphytum grandiflorum (comfrey)

Tellima grandiflora 'Purpurea'

Vaccinium vitis-idaea (cowberry)

Vinca major (periwinkle)

Vinca minor (lesser periwinkle)

Viola labradorica

Waldsteinia ternata

---

corners of your garden; you may prefer carpets of low growth or casual mounds of shrubs.

In a formal garden, though, where all is well ordered, such rampant growth can look odd. Here you will need plants which grow in a very neat way. The small-leaved ivies are a good choice, as they grow flat to the ground and can be kept within bounds by trimming the longer stems once a year.

Juniperus sabina 'Tamariscifolia' is a very well behaved juniper which grows into a neat flat-topped circle about 1.5m/5ft across and 45cm/18in high, looking as if it had been

When choosing ground cover to go beneath roses it is best to select plants that flower earlier or later than the roses. An added bonus is ground cover with contrasting foliage (above).

Rose of Sharon (below) spreads so fast that it can be a problem.

DRY SHADE

GARDEN NOTES

This is the most difficult to plant up. Dry shaded sites are commonly found under established trees and shrubs, where the tops shade the soil and the roots take all the moisture. New plants cannot compete.

One way of overcoming this is to use creeping or trailing plants and place them beyond the dry root zone. Once established, the ground cover plants should grow and spread into the difficult area. Use ivy, juniper, lamium or galeobdolon, which are all able to survive drought.

To help the new plants, fill their planting holes with garden compost or farmyard manure mixed in with soil to keep moisture in. Pour water into the hole before planting and water the plants well throughout their first year.

Photos Horticultural

trimmed each year, although this is not, in fact, necessary.

Other well-defined shapes which suit a formal garden are hostas, *Viburnum davidii* and *Prunus laurocerasus* 'Otto Luyken'. Geranium species also produce a confined mound of leaves and flowers.

For formal flower beds and borders, an underplanting of a mat-forming plant will take care of the weeds without distracting the eye from the main effect. For example, aubrieta or lamium would look good beneath roses.

Viburnum davidii (right) is an evergreen shrub that will produce an area of rich, dark green, weed-smothering cover. Its controlled form is ideal for formal-looking gardens. It prefers well-drained soils in sunny situations and is fully hardy. Each plant forms a clump about 90cm/3ft high and 1.5m/5ft wide. In late spring it has delicate white flowers and female forms produce metallic blue berries in autumn.

Photos Horticultural

PROJECT
PLANTING UP AN AREA

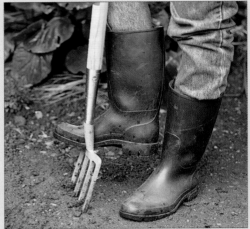

All Photos Marshall Cavendish

1 Fork over the ground, removing perennial weeds. If there is a lot of couch, bindweed or ground elder, hoe off the regrowth each week until the roots die. Or use a herbicide containing glyphosate.

2 Once weed free, level the soil with a rake, then tread the ground by walking on the balls of your feet. This gives the plants a firm soil to grow in. Rake the soil level to remove your footprints.

3 Set out your plants at the right spacing and plant them. If you water the plants well the day before, you will not have to water them in. If the ground is bone dry, pour water into the planting holes.

4 Apply a slow-release fertilizer to each plant so that it will establish itself quickly. To avoid future weeding lay a sheet of black polythene and plant into holes cut into it, or use a bark mulch.

AFTERCARE

Don't let your new plants dry out in the first year or two. It takes a while for them to put roots down into the deeper, damper soil and during the first years they are vulnerable to drought.

When it is very dry, water once a fortnight with a lot of water, rather than daily with a sprinkling. Gently apply about 4.5 litres/1 gall to each plant, 9 litres/2 gall to shrubs, so that you do not wash the soil away from the roots.

To speed growth, remember to feed the plants. Use a slow-release fertilizer, placed around each plant. Alternatively, water on a liquid feed to roots or leaves according to the instructions, in the spring and early summer.

Weeding is very important during the first few seasons. Use a hoe weekly to disturb weed seedlings before they are visible. Hand weed around plants with creeping growth that could be damaged by the hoe.

If you have used mulch to suppress the weeds, keep it topped up to its original depth to maintain its effectiveness.

DON'T FORGET!

Creating a Fern Garden

Hardy ferns, which are widely available from garden centres and through specialist mail order firms, can be used to create stylish shade gardens that are simultaneously cool and restful, yet relatively easy to look after.

Hardy ferns are the perfect answer for those difficult, damp, shady corners of the garden. You can grow them alone or with other plants to create a delightful and very fashionable fern garden.

Ferns are very collectable, as there are numerous unusual varieties. Though the range on offer in most garden centres is limited, lots more are available from mail order firms and specialist nurseries who advertise in the pages of gardening magazines.

When it comes to buying ferns, there is one major drawback. Very few have common names. For all but the most popular kinds, you will have to get to grips with the latin names. Write them down with a brief description before you go out plant-buying.

The best types to choose for a fern garden are medium-sized, ground covering kinds. There are dwarf ferns suitable for moist rock gardens, giants like the royal fern (*Osmunda regalis*), and species that grow well in dry-stone walls, but these are not really appropriate for a normal fern garden.

Planning a fern garden

There are three basic styles of fern garden. You can plant a range of fern species, chosen to make the most of the family's vast array of shapes and textures. Or you could plant a large drift of a single species. But the most popular way is to interplant ferns with other plants that thrive in shady and moist conditions.

Andrew Lawson

Ferns look best if they are planted to emphasize contrasts in shape and colour. Use evergreen ferns, such as hart's-tongue and *Polystichum* species, in groups as the basis of the planting scheme.

Hart's-tongue and the various crested forms of it are particularly useful. Their broad, glossy leaves make a strong contrast with the light, feathery foliage of species such as lady fern, male fern and soft shield fern.

Grow the hart's-tongue ferns in large groups, with smaller groups of feather ferns

A shady corner of a garden planted up with ferns and other shade-loving plants will prove to be a cool, restful place. The very different shapes of the vigorous fern sprays provide interesting contrasts.

Eric Crichton

A WILD GARDEN WITH FERNS

A selection of plants for creating a wild garden in a shady area.

Native fern species
Hart's-tongue
Lady fern
Male fern
Soft shield fern

Shade-loving wild flowers
Forget-me-not
Hardy cyclamen (*Cyclamen hederifolium*, syn. *neapolitanum*)
Primrose
Sweet woodruff (*Asperula odorata*)
Violet
Water avens (*Geum rivale*)

The bold, upright fronds of this fern (above), arching like the plumes of an ostrich, led to its common names of ostrich-feather fern or ostrich fern. Botanically it is known as Matteuccia struthiopteris. *The outer, fresh green fronds of this deciduous fern are sterile, hiding the inner, dark brown fertile fronds.*

The Japanese painted fern (Athyrium niponicum 'Pictum', also known as A. goeringianum) can have silver-blue fronds (right). A deciduous, hardy fern, it may succumb to severe winter weather.

Gillian Beckett

Pat Brindley

GOOD GARDEN FERNS			
Species	**Height**	**Appearance**	**Notes**
ADIANTUM			
Bird's-foot fern (A. pedatum)	20cm/8in	Neat fans of foliage	
Hardy maidenhair fern (A. venustum)	30cm/12in	Fragile, triangular sprays of pale green foliage	
ASPLENIUM			
Hart's-tongue fern A. scolopendrium	40cm/16in	Broad, evergreen, ribbon-like leaves	Chalk lover
Crested hart's-tongue (A. s. 'Cristatum')	40cm/16in	Broad, evergreen, crested leaves	Chalk lover
ATHYRIUM			
Lady fern (A. filix-femina)	70cm/28in	Tall lacy fronds	
Crested lady fern (A. f. Victoriae)	90cm/36in	Forms lattice of crested fronds	
Japanese painted fern (A. niponicum 'Pictum')	60cm/24in	Wine-red stems, silvery bronze leaves	Slightly tender
DRYOPTERIS			
D. erythrosora	50m/20in	Coppery pink new growth	
Curled male fern (D. filix-mas 'Crispa Cristata')	20cm/8in	Densely curled fronds	
Crested male fern (D. pseudo-mas 'Cristata The King')	90cm/36in	Tall, arching, crested fronds	Also called D. affinis
MATTEUCCIA			
Ostrich-feather fern (M. struthiopteris)	60cm/24in	Elegant large fern; shuttlecock-shaped plant; feathery foliage	Makes good specimen
POLYSTICHUM			
Soft shield fern (P. setiferum 'Divisilobum')	50cm/20in	Cut-leaved, evergreen fern; mound shaped, lacy foliage	

Ferns can be very attractively combined with other garden plants. Here (above left) clumps of fern are set among drifts of forget-me-nots on a slope beneath the bright green and red foliage of ornamental trees. The net result is very effective. Hart's tongue fern (Asplenium scolopendrium or Phyllitis scolopendrium) is an evergreen species whose distinctively shaped fronds (right) are eye-catching.

Eric Crichton

SHADE PLANTS TO GROW WITH FERNS

- Bugle (*Ajuga*): purple, reddish or variegated mats of foliage; blue flowers in spring.
- *Asarum caudatum*: heart-shaped, matt green leaves and brown flowers.
- *Asarum europaeum*: semi-evergreen, glossy, deep green, kidney-shaped leaves.
- Elephant's ears (*Bergenia*): large, rounded, glossy leaves, often reddening in autumn, and pink flowers in spring.
- *Epimedium* × *rubrum*: reddish foliage.
- *E. perralchicum* 'Fröhnleiten': yellow starry flowers and red-edged foliage.
- Hardy cranesbill (*Geranium phaeum*): small dusky-purple flowers.
- *Hosta* 'Gold Edger' or *H.* 'Ground Master': large, variegated leaves.
- Lily (*Lilium* 'Mabel Violet'): mauve, tinged white; scented.
- Tiger lily (*L. tigrinum*, syn. *lancifolium*): orange spotted.
- Toad lilies (*Tricyrtis* spp): yellow or mauve spotted flowers in late summer.
- Perennial forget-me-not (*Brunnera macrophylla*): blue flowers, large leaves.
- Solomon's seal (*Polygonatum multiflorum*) and its variegated form *P. multiflorum* 'Variegatum'.

in among them or slightly in front of them. Add a single ostrich-feather fern as a focal point. A mulch of bark chippings around it will make it even more distinctive.

It is a good idea to add a few 'hard' features. Logs, tree stumps or a group of rocks will break up the carpet of foliage.

Hard features provide a good backdrop for the colourful foliage of Japanese painted fern or *Dryopteris erythrosora*. Both of these ferns look less spectacular against a background of matt green.

Using one species

A single species fern garden looks particularly effective as ground cover under trees. It

Eric Crichton

looks equally good in a shady situation against a background of large mature shrubs, particularly varieties with striking foliage colours and shapes. Drifts of a single species in shade under trees will 'cool down' a very colourful distant view.

A mixed planting

A fern and shade plant garden offers the best possibilities from the design point of view. Hardy ferns contrast particularly well with shade- and moisture-loving herbaceous plants, especially those with striking shapes.

Dot groups of taller ferns between carpets of low-growing ground cover plants, and include occasional clumps of taller plants for variety.

Cultivating ferns

Hardy ferns need a site in full or dappled shade, with a fertile, moisture-retentive soil. If

the ground is not sufficiently moist, dig in lots of well-rotted organic material.

Fork in old farmyard manure, garden compost or coco-fibre, but avoid mushroom compost. This contains chalk and many, though not all, hardy ferns prefer soil which is neutral or slightly acid.

Container-grown ferns can be planted at any season. The best time, though, is early spring as they start into growth. Knock plants carefully from their containers and plant without disturbing the root-ball. However, do tease out a few large roots if the pot is tightly packed; this will give the plant a better start.

After planting, water them in well and then mulch with a 3-5cm/1-2in layer of chipped bark. This may seem expensive, but it lasts for many years without needing a top up, unlike mulches of peat or cocofibre, which break down

David Squire

Soft shield fern (Polystichum setiferum) *coated with frost (left). It is an evergreen or semi-evergreen. It can be propagated by spores or by division in spring, or by potting up the plantlets which appear on fronds in autumn.*

Male fern (Dryopteris filix-mas) *is an elegant fern (top), suitable for a larger border. It grows to about 1.2m/4ft in height.*

The bright flowers of geraniums (above) contrast well with the vivid green of ostrich-feather fern.

PROJECT

GROW FERNS FROM SPORES

1 *Collect mature fronds in late summer when the capsules containing spores form dark patterns on the undersides of the leaves.*

3 *Prepare some sterilized seed compost, heating it in the oven at 50°C for one hour. When cool put it in a clean container without holes.*

Marshall Cavendish

2 *Hang fronds in paper bags in a cool airy place to dry. When the spores fall to the bottom of the bag they are ready for sowing.*

4 *Scatter the spores over moist compost, fit the lid, and leave in a cool shady place. Check occasionally to see if watering is needed.*

Anytime from one to 18 months after sowing the spores, minute, green, algae-like growths should appear. These will eventually produce tiny ferns, which should be pricked off into trays of sterilized compost and kept moist beneath cling film. When big enough to handle, harden off and pot up singly.

Eric Crichton

and need annual additions.

Chipped bark not only conserves moisture in the soil and smothers out weed seedlings, it also creates an attractive background against which ferns and other shade lovers show up well.

Routine care of a fern gar-den is negligible. Make sure plants are kept watered when first planted. Water them, too, during a prolonged drought, even when they are well es-tablished, since ferns need moist conditions.

Cut dead fronds of decidu-ous species back to ground level in late autumn. In cold areas, leave this job until early spring. In the meantime, bend the dead fronds over the crown of the plant to protect it from the worst effects of frost.

Unlike most garden plants, ferns cannot be grown from cuttings. By far the best way to propagate them is by divid-ing up large clumps in early spring or late autumn.

Propagation

Use two forks back to back and an old knife to cut through dense clumps of root. After im-proving the soil with more or-ganic matter and a handful of general purpose fertilizer, re-plant the best pieces. Discard old sections from the centre of the clump. Commercially, har-dy ferns are raised from spores. This is a slow process but it can be quite fun to try at home (see project box).

Clothing Slopes and Banks

Garden areas on sloping sites can be difficult to maintain, but a creative approach to planting can transform this problem into a design opportunity.

Derek Gould

Many gardens are laid out on fairly uniform, level sites, but even these may feature a steep slope near an entrance drive or on a road frontage. Others may be set into hillsides, with a variety of slopes and banks.

If the slope is a gentle one, you will probably find it is simplest to sow grass seed or to turf it. However, steeper slopes can be difficult to mow.

If a steep bank is left unplanted, you will be faced with the possibility of soil being eroded in windy conditions or washing away in heavy rains. In this situation, you may have to consider the expensive option of building retaining walls to hold the bank in place. While this may be costly in terms of labour and materials, it may suit your long-term needs best.

Design options

Very hilly sites can be rebuilt as a series of terraces, adding distinctive areas of interest to the garden. Reduce the slope's

If you have to garden on a very hilly site, there may be no choice other than to build retaining walls and create a series of terraces (above). On a smaller scale, a slope may be transformed by digging out and lining a stream, fed by a pump, and surrounding it with suitable rocks and plants (right). The simplest, and certainly the cheapest option is to clothe a bank with plants such as aubrieta (above right).

Photos Horticultural

Douglas Knight/Garden Picture Library

gradient in stages so that you can use the soil from one level to backfill another level. This keeps the expense of removing waste soil from the site to a minimum.

If the slope is not too steep, and can be easily maintained, you can use formal herbaceous borders to break it up and provide interesting accents. The beds themselves will make the change in level and you will not have to do any major construction work.

Rocks and water

For really dramatic results, you can emphasize a slope by incorporating a natural looking garden feature. Water features, such as a cascade or a stream ending in a tranquil pool, will make the best use of a difficult to maintain slope. Preformed cascades are obtainable in kit form from water garden centres.

Use some of the soil from the excavations to make a rock garden along the length of the waterway.

GARDEN NOTES

SHRUBS AND CLIMBERS

Brooms, including *Cytisus × kewensis* with its arching stems and creamy-white, late spring flowers and Spanish broom (*Genista hispanica*), can be pegged down to make good cover.

The low-growing and evergreen *Arctostaphylos uva-ursi* has tiny bell-like flowers, followed by berries. Prostrate cotoneasters such as 'Skogholm' provide good autumn foliage and berry interest, as well as spring flowers.

Climbers for a sunny slope include the Chilean trumpet vine (*Campsis radicans*) and the everlasting sweet pea (*Lathyrus latifolius*). The honeysuckle *Lonicera japonica* 'Halliana' also performs well on a sunny bank or slope.

Harry Smith Collection

Rockeries themselves can be used instead of herbaceous beds to break up a slope. Stones and scree set into the slope look natural and make an attractive backdrop for alpine plants, which appreciate the free drainage of a hilly site. Mulch the planted rockery with gravel or bark to keep it weed-free while the relatively slow-growing plants form an integrated ground cover.

Using plants

With luck, you will be able to deal with a slope without any major construction work. Plants are your best allies in

GARDEN NOTES

FLAT CONIFERS

For low maintenance, there are several evergreen and ground-covering junipers to choose from. For fresh spring green, use *Juniperus communis* 'Hornibrookii' and 'Prostrata'. For a blue effect choose *J. squamata* 'Blue Carpet'.

this. Ground-covering plants like ivy or prostrate cotoneaster provide practical, as well as ornamental value. Their roots stabilize and hold the soil. As they grow they offer attractive leaf colour and shape. Other plants, such as low-growing roses, will provide additional ornament with their flowers.

You can cover a bank with just one type of plant for ease of maintenance, but the effect may be a little dull. Mixed plantings are more ornamental and offer you the opportunity to find complementary plants that provide long-term seasonal interest.

Sun or shade

The site and soil type of the bank will determine your choice of plants. For full sun, there are a wide range of shrubs, herbs and sun-loving grey-leaved plants to choose from. Rock roses (helianthemums) and broom make an attractive combination for a sunny bank, as do aromatic

herbs such as thyme, sage and prostrate rosemary (*Rosmarinus lavandulacens*). This form of rosemary needs a sunny, sheltered site as it is not always hardy.

Chamomile will make a wonderfully scented cover for such a site. Keeping it trim in spring and summer makes a

Azaleas and rhododendrons grow on mountainous sites in the wild and will happily take to a slope if given an acid soil (above). Prostrate conifers, such as Juniperus squamata 'Blue Carpet' (below) provide good, low-maintenance cover for a bank.

Pat Brindley

Eric Crichton

Retaining walls will benefit from being softened by tumbling plants (above). Here, two varieties of Alyssum saxatile *syn.* Aurinia saxatalis, *the buff 'Dudley Neville' and lemony 'Citrina' combine with the snow-white* Iberis sempervirens *to make a late spring show.*

A terraced garden needs to incorporate steps if it is to be enjoyed to the full. These should fit harmoniously with the rest of the garden. Here (below) the terraces are linked by a formal flight made of the same stone as the retaining walls.

pleasantly fragrant task. If the scented bank is not too steep, you could cut a place out of it to make a seat.

In a shady situation, especially if the soil is fairly moist, you can create a damp woodland garden for ferns and primulas. Other options for such a site include bergenia, hostas, trillium and *Helleborus orientalis*.

The golden-flowered rose of Sharon (*Hypericum calycinum*) grows well in sunshine and shade. Plant patches of variegated leaf ivy or periwinkle among it to give a different colour accent.

Ornamental grasses and low-growing bamboos will offer architectural shape and variety of colour. Their mound-forming growth habit will eventually keep the ground weed-free.

If your garden soil is acid, use the bank to make a rhododendron and azalea dell. Alternatively, heathers and prostrate conifers will make a good display, hold the soil and keep it weed-free.

If a slope takes your eye to a ditch or stream, use the most natural plants for the situation. Cowslips, bluebells and primroses will all spread to make good cover and provide flowers in spring. Maintain

the bank in summer, after the plants have seeded, by scything down any invasive grasses or weeds.

Bronze-purple with green edges, the foliage of purple clover (*Trifolium repens* 'Purpurascens') makes a dense mat for a wild bank. It has white flowers through the summer and is semi-evergreen.

Paths and steps

To get access to maintain the bank, or to reach another level in the garden, you need steps or a pathway. If the setting is informal, use log steps or old railway sleepers as risers to hold the soil in place. Cover the treads of the step area with gravel or a thick layer of bark mulch. For a more formal look, use frost-proof bricks or natural stone pavers to make the steps.

If you need to move a mower or wheelbarrow to a different level of the garden consider a winding, not-too-steeply graded ramp. Cobbles, bricks or gravel give an attractive surface; bricks are best if you are going to have to push heavy loads up the ramp.

If you are working on a previously unplanted site, you will need to carry out a little

Tania Midgley

MOW HOW

Grass can be excellent cover for a sloping site, provided the gradient is not too steep, no more than 1 in 4 (25%). Steeper sites are difficult to maintain.

If the slope is gentle enough to mow, there are still safety precautions you must take. It is best to use a wheeled mower, either a cylinder or rotary model.

Always work at right angles, across the slope. Never push the machine uphill – it may run backwards onto your feet. Mowing downhill also has its dangers, as the machine could gain momentum and run away, perhaps taking you with it.

SAFETY FIRST

preparation. Use a systemic weedkiller to clean out weeds. You can fork or dig them out, but take care not to disturb the soil overmuch.

Planting the bank

The soil may need enriching with a dressing of topsoil before you begin. Always work your way down from the top of the slope, and when you begin to plant, work across the slope.

You may need to protect the top soil, holding it in place before the plants get established. Use various mulching materials to do this. Black plastic sheeting, close-mesh netting or a thick straw layer are all suitable. Make slits in the black plastic and holes in the netting for individual plants.

If the site is dry and windswept, make sure that individual plants have a little hollow around them to collect water.

Once the plants are well-established, they will need little attention except for routine seasonal care. In drought conditions some may need extra water. When flowering is over, trim back plants such as heathers and thymes.

Grass has both advantages and disadvantages on a sloping site. It is very effective in preventing soil erosion and provides an attractive backdrop for other planting, but can be difficult to maintain. For relatively shallow slopes, however, it is ideal (above).

Rocks can make a very informal type of terraced garden, with pockets of flat ground suitable for spring bulbs (left), as well as more conventional rockery plants.

Filling the Gaps

Do your paving slabs look bare, your old stone paths have unsightly cracks? Bring them to life with some attractive plants that love to grow in gaps.

Do not despair if your paving is starting to crack and look shabby. Revitalize it with plants and turn it into a stunning garden feature.

If the cracks are not very large make them bigger with a cold chisel and hammer (don't be alarmed — it's really quite easy). Aim for cracks about 2.5-5cm/1-2in wide and deep enough to reach the soil below — 15cm/6in would be a good depth. Then fill the cracks with soil or compost such as John Innes No 2.

Going crazy
You may already have an area that is crazy paved — and this, of course, is ideal for planting. If the joins are filled with mortar that is cracking, break it up here and there, using a knife. Remove the broken pieces of mortar and fill the gaps with soil or compost.

These cracks and crevices can then become home to a wide range of colourful and interesting plants. Those that like well-drained or dry conditions are generally used and most are sun lovers.

You need not limit yourself to these plants, however, as there are also a few moisture-loving plants that are suitable (provided you can keep the soil or compost fairly damp). Also, there are several types of plants that enjoy being in light shade.

Dwarf plant types are generally best for filling gaps in paving. By far the majority of suitable plants are alpines or rock plants. Often they have an interesting habit of growth

Peter McHoy

and are mat or cushion forming. Some hardy perennials or small shrubs are also suitable.

Get rid of weeds
Before attempting to plant up a paved area it is vital to kill all perennial weeds. These thrive in cracks and crevices and are awkward to remove completely by hand. The only

effective way to deal with stubborn weeds is to kill them at the roots which can be done by applying a weedkiller containing glyphosate, during the growing season.

Filling the cracks
You could use ordinary garden soil to fill the cracks prior to planting, provided it is not

An ordinary flight of steps is transformed by a glorious garland of campanula. Cunningly planted in the gap between the wall and the step this clever carpeter makes its way downstairs and crawls into the cracks.

Eric Crichton

Peter McHoy

Harry Smith

heavy clay, but a soil-based potting compost would tend to produce better results. Whatever soil or compost you use, add one-third extra of horticultural grit to ensure it remains well aerated and drained.

The soil or compost must be pushed well into the cracks and crevices – in fact, to their extremities. Use a stick with a rounded end if necessary. The aim is to avoid an air pocket in the growing medium, otherwise plants will not root properly. Do not water the compost before planting, as it is much easier to fill cracks in paving if the soil is dry.

Choosing the plants

Choose plants that are small so you can fit them easily in to cracks and crevices. Many of the plants listed, especially the alpines, may be available in 8cm/3in pots.

When to grow

It is best to plant in early to mid spring although if conditions are mild and dryish early autumn is fine. If it is very cold or wet, or if you live in a chilly area it is better to stick to planting in spring.

If you buy plants in pots, carefully tease some of the soil away from the roots. On no account try to cram roots into the cracks – it is better to remove some more soil.

In a paved area, use a narrow-bladed trowel to dig a hole sufficiently deep to allow the roots to hang down to their

Old crazy paving in a well established garden (above left) has been given a new lease of life with these bright and cheerful plants. Thyme not only adds a dash of colour, it is also aromatic.

The chance meeting of these two flowers has produced such a harmonious effect against the severe rock background that they have been left to grow naturally.

Harry Smith

Insight Picture Library

If you tread the path to the garden seat (above), the wonderfully aromatic carpeters will release their perfumes.

This collection of plants (left) is ideal for filling cracks in paving. Bright yellow saxifrage partners well with snow-in-summer. The miniature rose adds a delicate touch.

The eye catching herringbone brick work (left) has been laid with gaps so that moss can easily self seed and spread to become part of the intricate design. The striking contrast of the green border draws out the mottled colours in the bricks themselves.

PLANT PROPAGATION

You can use small rooted divisions and offsets of your own plants or cuttings from friends' gardens. Many alpines and hardy perennials can be increased by division in spring. Offset-producing plants include *sempervivums*. Most shrubby plants can be propagated from cuttings. Allow the new roots to develop well before planting into paving.

full extent. If there is not enough room even for a narrow trowel, use a stick with a rounded end, then trickle fine soil around the roots and firm it in thoroughly.

Sowing seeds

Dwarf hardy and half-hardy annuals can also be grown from seed in between paving to provide summer colour.

It is a comparatively easy matter to sow seeds in the cracks, but do try to sow as thinly as possible to minimize thinning out of seedlings, then cover seeds lightly with fine soil or compost. Keep them well watered until the seeds have begun to sprout.

Hardy annuals may be sown during early or mid spring, but wait to sow half-hardy kinds until late spring when the danger of frost is past.

Easy maintenance

In the main, these dwarf plants are compact and need little in the way of tidying, except perhaps to remove dead flowers. Several spreading varieties are improved by being trimmed back lightly after flowering. This maintains a neat shape and encourages new growth.

Most of the plants in the list (overleaf) establish themselves quite rapidly. They soon make an attractive display, so giving a mature look to a newly paved area or fresh interest to tired old paving. Remember that the compost or soil in cracks and crevices will dry out rapidly during warm weather, so keep an eye on it and water as necessary. The best way to apply water is to use a garden sprinkler or a watering can with a fine rose.

An infusion of pink thrift with its mass of pretty flower heads (right) gives a lift to this dull, grey stone wall. Planted carefully in the crack between the rocks it grows diagonally up the slope retaining its soft cushion shape.

Eric Crichton

This beautiful bellflower (left) drapes elegantly over a rugged collection of rocks, softening the harsh edges and introducing colour as it grows. The romantic bluish-purple hues and exquisite star-shaped flowers make an eye-catching feature.

This sunny alyssum (below) is a happy resident of a wall, cascading beautifully over the edge. The multitude of bright yellow pompon flower heads will give bright colour in springtime.

Eric Crichton

PROJECT   PLANTING IN PAVING

Plan ahead by getting rid of weeds (it is better to use a weedkiller as it is difficult to make sure you have removed all the roots by hand). Find out the mature size of your plants in order to work out planting distances. Here, saxifrages, campanulas and sempervivums have been chosen to provide a succession of flowers from spring until late summer. Alyssum can be grown from seed and so it is easy to sow in crevices; it will also self seed in following seasons. Unlike camomile and thyme which, when stepped on, give off an aroma, these plants should not be planted where people are likely to tread.

Ray Duns

1 Make a space larger than pla roots. Add a little compost, ins plant, fill hole with more comp

Photos Horticultural

GOOD GAP FILLERS

BLUES

Bellflower: summer, spreading habit.
Globularia *(G. cordifolia):* summer, mat-forming habit.
Violet cress: blue-tinged flowers, summer annual.
Baby blue eyes: blue and white, summer, hardy annual.
Horned violet: spring-summer, spreading clumps.

FOLIAGE

Corsican mint: tiny aromatic leaves, creeping.
Stonecrop: fleshy grey purplish rosettes, mat-forming.
Cobweb houseleek: webbed rosettes.

MULTI-COLOURED

Livingstone daisy: summer, half-hardy annual.
Sun plant *(Portulaca grandiflora):* summer, half-hardy annual.

PINKS AND REDS

New Zealand burr: spiny red seed heads, mat-forming habit.
Stone cress *(Aethionema):* 'Warley Rose', pink flowers, spring-summer, compact.
Thrift: pink flowers, late spring, cushion-forming.
Maiden pink: summer, mat-forming habit.
Alpine fleabane, summer, clump-forming.
Stork's bill: summer, hummock-forming.
Cranesbill *(Geranium dalmaticum):* summer, prostrate.
Baby's breath *(Gypsophila repens):* white or pink flowers, summer, prostrate.

This small, spreading alpine saxifrage (left), flowers in early spring. The unusual spiky clump formed by this species, S. × apiculata, is refined by the simple, graceful, yellow flowers.

This attractive bright pink thyme (right) has hundreds of tiny flowers which are beautifully scented and are particularly attractive to bees. This common variety is called Thymus serpyllum.

Eric Crichton

Making sure all weeds have ~n removed, fill cracks with ~mpost and sow seeds sparingly.

3 Carefully add a thin layer of grit round the base of plants and over seeds. Water seeds regularly.

Peter McHoy

'irginian stock: pink, white or red, self sows freely, hardy annual.
>rimula 'Wanda': crimson-purple flowers, spring, clump-forming.
>oapwort: pink flowers, summer, mat-forming.
Noss campion (Saponaria ocymoides): spring, hummock-forming.
hyme (T. lanuginosus): summer, aromatic foliage, mat-forming.

YELLOWS

arrow: yellow flowers, summer, mat-forming.
Nlyssum (A. montanum): yellow flowers, early spring prostrate habit.
>room (Cytisus ardoinii): late spring, hummock-forming.
Nlpine wallflowers: late spring, bushy habit.
>t. John's wort (Hypericum olympicum): yellow flowers, summer, bushy.
>oached-egg flower: white and yellow flowers, summer, hardy annual.
Norisia monanthos: late spring-early summer, prostrate rosettes.
>inquefoil (Potentilla x tonguei): summer, mat-forming.
>axifrage x apiculata: light yellow flowers, early spring, cushion-forming habit.
hyme (T. praecox): tiny aromatic leaves, prostrate.

WHITES

Naiden pink: summer, mat-forming habit.
Nountain avens: late spring, mat-forming.
>tork's bill: summer, hummock-forming.
>aby's breath (Gypsophila repens): summer, prostrate.
>hamois cress (Hutchinsia alpina): late spring-summer, tufted habit.
>andytuft (Iberis saxatilis): spring-early summer, bushy.
>delweiss: white flowers surrounded by grey bracts, spring, tufted.
Norned violet: spring-summer, spreading.

Raising their cheerful faces to the sun, these Livingstone daisies (above) are well adapted to growing in the smallest of cracks and crevices. They grow to 15cm/6in high and have a spreading habit which enables them to grow over rugged terrain.

A slightly taller addition to the gaps in your paving could be these modern pinks. They grow to 37cm/15in and are faster growing than their relatives in the dianthus family. In very mild weather they may flower right up until mid-winter.

Brian Carter/Garden Picture Library

Choosing Seaside Plants

A seaside garden can be a headache or a haven, depending on whether the coast is windswept or sheltered and mild. It pays to know what to grow.

Eric Crichton

Seaside gardens, and the plants that grow in them, vary enormously, depending on their geographical situation and the local micro-climate. At one extreme they can be almost sub-tropical, while at the other, on cold, exposed coasts, even the toughest native plants find it hard to prosper without shelter.

If you have just moved to a coastal region, the first step is to look at what other people choose to grow in your area.

Join the local gardening club and talk to members about what grows well for them. And take the opportunity to visit as many nearby gardens as you can.

They will be full of interesting plants and ideas for planting them together. As you gain experience, you will soon know which are worth trying in your own garden.

Do not be afraid to experiment with unknown plants – it is all part of the fun. And don't necessarily avoid those that may be on the borderline of hardiness in your site. You can always keep a few rooted cuttings on a window-sill in winter for security.

Shelter belts

While you are surveying local gardens, get the next phase under way. This is to establish a good shelter belt round the

A group of holm oaks shelter a sunny rock garden of bright blooms (left), not far from the sea. A sheltered, sunken location like this can be mild and many plants will flourish.

The fast-growing Monterey pine (right) has attractive flowers and grows to form an excellent windbreak.

Tamarisk (below) forms broad, pink-flowered hedges that break the wind in exposed situations.

This variety of sycamore (bottom) is 'Brilliantissimum'. Its leaves develop from salmon-pink to yellow and then turn dark green. It is a good shelter belt tree.

Brian Carter/Garden Picture Library

Eric Crichton

PLANTS FOR EXPOSED SITUATIONS

The following plants will survive on exposed coasts and are ideal for shelter belts.

TREES
Sycamore (*Acer pseudoplatanus*): deciduous.
Hawthorn (*Crataegus* species): deciduous, spring flowers, autumn berries.
White poplar (*Populus alba*): deciduous, rustles in the wind.
Whitebeam (*Sorbus aria*): deciduous, small white flowers, red berries.
Swedish whitebeam (*Sorbus intermedia*): deciduous, small white flowers, red berries.
Holm oak (*Quercus ilex*): evergreen oak.
Corsican pine (*Pinus nigra maritima*): evergreen conifer.
Monterey pine (*Pinus radiata*): evergreen conifer.

SHRUBS
Bamboo (*Arundinaria* species): semi-evergreen.
Sea purslane (*Atriplex halimus*): semi-evergreen, silvery-grey leaves.
Elaeagnus ebbingei: evergreen, leathery leaves with silvery undersides.
Escallonia macrantha: evergreen, pink flowers all summer and into autumn.
Sea buckthorn (*Hippophae rhamnoides*): deciduous, silvery willow-like leaves, orange berries if both sexes grown.
Daisy bush (*Olearia* × *haastii*): evergreen, white daisy flowers.
Pyracantha species: evergreen, red, orange or yellow berries.
Rosa rugosa varieties: deciduous rose, large hips.
Rosa pimpinellifolia: deciduous, creamy-white flowers.
Senecio 'Sunshine': evergreen, silver foliage, yellow flowers.
Tamarisk (*Tamarix pentandra*): deciduous, pink flowers in late summer.
Gorse (*Ulex europaeus*): appears evergreen, yellow flowers from spring through to late winter.

Collections/Patrick Johns

edge of the garden.

If you are lucky enough to benefit from the shelter of trees and bushes in surrounding gardens, or planted along roadside verges, don't rely on them – they may be cut down.

To take the brunt of the blast, plant an 'outer defence' of trees, shrubs or a tall hedge, choosing plants that are both salt- and wind-tolerant.

Plant trees in staggered rows, and stake them securely for the first few years until they are established. Ideally, you should plant a border of shrubs inside the belt of trees, for extra protection.

If your garden is small, avoid trees and go for a hedge of hawthorn or *Escallonia macrantha*, or a wide border thickly planted with a mixture of the more tolerant shrubs.

Within the area protected by your shelter belt, you can quite easily grow a surprisingly wide range of moderately tolerant garden plants.

Coastwise plants

Trees like birch, holly and eucalyptus will thrive. So will shrubs like juniper, aucuba, buddleia, choisya, cistus, cotoneaster, fuchsia, *Hebe salicifolia*, hypericum, ribes, rosemary, willows and laurustinus (*Viburnum tinus*).

For low hedges, grow the honeysuckles *Lonicera pileata* and *L. nitida*. Both can be quite tightly clipped, and they regenerate quickly if they do get knocked back by a salty blow once in a while.

Among flowers, you will find that pinks (*Dianthus* species), erigeron and mallows do well, even right on the coast. In a windy garden, alpines will thrive. They don't mind breezy conditions so long as they are sheltered from salt-laden winds coming off the sea.

In mild, well sheltered gardens, any number of slightly tender trees, shrubs and climbers can be grown (see box). You can also try exotics like the ginger lily (*Hedychium gardnerianum*), and a huge range of fascinating, subtropical summer bedding.

The coastal environment has some problems that inland gardeners may not experience. In summer, for instance, coastal gardens may be very dry, since it is generally hotter and brighter close to the sea.

Coastal problems

Greenhouses may need to be shaded earlier in the year than in inland gardens. They may also need an extra coat of shading paint in midsummer to combat the strong sunlight.

Try to site greenhouses so they are sheltered from salt-laden sea-breezes. If this is not possible, place the ventilators on the side away from the sea, to minimize salt damage to plants inside.

South-facing conservatories are likely to become too hot for comfort, both for plants and people. It is generally best to have a conservatory that faces east or west.

Seaside gardens are likely to remain breezy, even in summer. Herbaceous plants, therefore, will probably need more staking. Shorter varieties, that would not be staked inland, may well need support. Climbing plants, too, will need to be firmly secured.

Choosing evergreens

Certain evergreens are unsuitable as windbreaks. In areas with strong winds that carry

Don Wildridge

salt, everyday hedging conifers, like Leyland's cypress and yew, go totally brown within a day or two of storm-free winds.

Evergreen shrubs like privet also suffer in the same way, and will remain brown and leafless until new growth appears in spring. Conifers, however, invariably remain stubbornly brown on the windward side, and never replace their dead foliage.

The best remedy is to remove the plants and replace them with salt-tolerant conifers or evergreens. Alternatively, you could grow a border of suitable coastal plants in front of them to hide the damaged brown foliage.

Wind-burn

In windy areas, it is a mistake to plant shrubs that flower early in the spring – the wind just burns the buds off almost as soon as they open.

Flowering trees, such as lilac and ornamental cherry, are also best avoided unless you have a very sheltered spot.

Photos Horticultural

Gillian Beckett

TENDER PLANTS FOR WARM, SHELTERED SITUATIONS

TREES
Eucryphia species: small trees, large white flowers in summer.
New Zealand lancewood tree (*Pseudopanax crassifolius*): striking evergreen, branches take years to appear.
Chusan palm (*Trachycarpus fortunei*): evergreen, frost hardy palm.

SHRUBS
Lobster claw (*Clianthus puniceus*): evergreen or semi-evergreen wall shrub, long bunches of claw-like red flowers.
Wire-netting bush (*Corokia cotoneaster*): evergreen, stems form wire-netting pattern.
Lantern tree (*Crinodendron hookerianum*): evergreen, bright red lantern-like flowers.
Pineapple broom (*Cytisus battandieri*): semi-evergreen wall shrub, large yellow flower-heads, strong pineapple scent.
Fremontodendron californicum: evergreen or semi-evergreen wall shrub, large single yellow flowers.
Broadleaf (*Griselinia littoralis*): very salt-resistant evergreen shrub, pale green leathery leaves.
Mount Etna broom (*Genista aetnensis*): spectacular tree broom with yellow flowers in summer.
Hebe species: small evergreen shrubs, short flower spikes in pink, mauve or white in mid to late summer.
Helichrysum plicatum: evergreen, bright silver shrub with needle-like leaves.
Tea tree (*Leptospermum* species): small evergreen shrubs, waxy pink flowers in summer.
Honeybush (*Melianthus major*): striking evergreen shrub, silvery-green foliage shaped like Prince of Wales feathers.
Olearia macrodonta: large evergreen shrub, very salt resistant, silvery-green holly-shaped leaves.
Pittosporum species: large evergreen shrubs, foliage (which can be variegated) is popular with flower arrangers.

The four plants here are exotic-looking species that will flourish in warm, sheltered sites where there is protection from strong, salt-laden winds. The chusan or fan palm (top left) is hardy enough to survive in a temperate climate. It produces yellow flowers in early summer. The pineapple broom (left) has pineapple-scented flowers in late spring or early summer. The lantern tree (above) from Chile grows to a height of 3-4.5m/10-15ft. Its red flowers appear in spring and early summer. Honeybush (right) looks good in a shrub border with its unusual foliage and long red-brown flowers.

Eric Crichton

Even though they flower later in the spring, it can still be very windy. Your flowers will almost certainly be blown off or turned brown within a day or two of opening.

Fruit trees, especially early flowering kinds like peaches, can also be a disaster for the same reason. If the flowers are browned by wind, insects will not visit to pollinate them and there will be no crop. Choosing late-flowering varieties is much safer – any good fruit catalogue will tell you exactly which these are.

As a general rule, wall-trained fruit trees survive in windy areas better than trees growing in the open, as the wall provides some shelter. For the same reason, slightly tender trees or shrubs are best grown against a wall.

Eucryphia glutinosa (left) is a flowering tree which can grow to over 9m/30ft. It is a deciduous species which may be spreading or upright in habit. The large, fragrant white flowers are borne from midsummer to late summer. Its glossy leaves turn orange-red in autumn. It is frost hardy but needs a sheltered situation, ideally with its roots in moist shade and its crown in sunshine. The soil must be lime-free and fertile.

The tea tree from New Zealand is an evergreen shrub with dramatic sprays of flowers in late spring and summer. The variety here (below) is 'Red Damask'. In cold areas it should be planted against a wall.

Photos Horticultural

USING SEAWEED

Seaweed is a very useful source of bulky organic material, providing potash and many valuable trace elements.

Collect your seaweed and – away from the garden – wash the worst of the salt off with a hose. Then either dig it into ground you will be planting in spring, such as the vegetable garden, or compost it.

Beetroot and asparagus will both tolerate salt in the soil, so unwashed seaweed can be dug in where they are to grow. You can also use neat seaweed to mulch an asparagus bed in spring or autumn.

The best way to compost seaweed is to place it in layers, alternating seaweed with lawn mowings, or kitchen peelings.

Seaweed speeds up the rotting of straw-based manure; place alternate layers in a heap or compost bin. The mixture should be ready for use in six months.

GO ORGANIC!

Don Wildridge

Creating a Miniature Garden

Short of space? By using compact plants, you can create an entire landscape in miniature. Perfect for an interesting feature or, in a tiny plot, a whole garden.

This miniature railway has been lovingly set in a miniature landscape at Babbacombe Model Village in Devon. The railway itself and the model people are perfectly in scale with a hillside 'wood', tiny golf course and parkland. Much of the effect is achieved by trimming tiny shrubs into the shapes of mature trees.

Peter McHoy

Enthusiasts have created miniature landscapes for nearly two centuries. The Victorians made rockeries that were virtually scale models of parts of the Alps, correct in every detail right down to the lookout points and telescopes. The creators of miniature villages, like the famous one in the English Cotswolds, surrounded their tiny houses with gardens on the same scale, for authenticity. And garden railway fans have for many years built, not only scale-model track layouts running round their gardens, but also very detailed miniature landscapes to 'naturalize' them.

Nowadays, many gardeners are turning to miniaturized gardens both to keep up with fashions, and to make the best use of space.

Changing trends

In large gardens, the current trend is away from wide open vistas, and increasingly towards dividing the space up into smaller, more intimate, 'gardens within gardens'. One of these could well be a miniature garden. If you are a compulsive designer, you could create a series of miniature gardens within a large plot.

But in a pocket handkerchief-sized space, you can turn the whole area into a miniature garden – the style is tailor-made for it. By using lots of fine detail, you can enjoy watching an ever-changing pattern of plants unfold in front of your windows all year.

Proportion and scale

Even though you probably do not want to create a true 'scale model' garden, it is important to keep an eye on the proportions if you want your miniature landscape to look right.

The smaller the space, the smaller the plants you will need. But it is also important to choose plants that are in proportion to each other. It is no good, for instance, mixing shrubs that are simply compact with those that are positively miniature – they just will not go well together. So decide early on which you want, and check ultimate plant heights and spreads when you buy.

Choosing plants

Anybody can create a small garden from small plants. But if you are making a real miniature garden, the trick lies in finding plants that give the same effect as a full-sized plant, but on a smaller scale. There are miniature versions of many popular garden plants – think of dwarf rhododendrons and conifers, miniature narcissi and roses, edging box, and so on, which are found in most garden centres. (As a rough guide, anything with a latin name ending in the word *nana* or *pygmea* will be a small version of the original plant).

There are also a good many flowers that are specially bred to be compact versions of tra-

DESIGN TIPS

- In designing your miniature garden, follow the same guidelines as for planning a normal garden, but using smaller plants chosen to provide the same sort of effects – eg seasonal colour, variation in plant shape and height, contrasts of texture and so on.
- Don't try to be too clever with the design. The result should be instantly recognizable as a complete garden in miniature. But unlike a conventional garden which is usually seen from one direction, remember a miniature garden will be viewed from above as well.
- Keep everything in the garden to a similar scale. Avoid mixing ultra dwarf varieties with those that are merely compact, or the result will look odd.
- Take trouble over detail. It is fun hunting out 'scaled down' accessories like containers, ornaments and even gravel (try the sort sold for fish tanks) to complete the scene.
- Don't try to miniaturize full-sized trees, shrubs and roses by cutting them back hard – they won't flower, and instead produce thickets of vigorous suckers.
- Try to avoid having a lawn; they never really look in scale. If necessary, go for a 'lawn' of pearlwort or moss (which need well compacted soil and moist, slightly shaded conditions), or the dwarf creeping thyme (*Thymus serpyllum* 'Minimus') in a sunny dryish spot. Or you could use fine (ryegrass-free) lawn seed and keep the grass cut very closely.

Derek Gould

ditionally tall plants, such as many newer varieties of sunflowers, delphiniums, asters, and other flowers which are often only one-third normal height. (You can grow from seed, though many compact perennials can be had from mail order plant catalogues).

In a very restricted space, even dwarf versions of 'normal' plants can be too big, so in some circumstances you may need to cheat a bit. Many rock plants, for instance, can be

Low-growing plants (above), especially those that form clumps and can be trimmed into desired shapes, are invaluable in a mini landscape. They can be shaped to resemble trees or bushes, and flowering species can look like beds of full-sized annuals. The plants here are a dwarf conifer, thymes, Dianthus, violas, saxifrage and sempervivum.

FIRST STEPS

If you are new to garden design and do not feel confident of creating a pretty garden at the first attempt, do not plant your miniature garden straight away. Since the plants are naturally small, they should be quite happy left in pots for the first year. Instead, simply 'plunge' them, pot and all, into prepared ground. That way, you can easily lift and reposition plants until you are quite happy with the layout, before planting them properly. In the same way, any new plants you are adding to the garden can be 'plunged' temporarily while you decide where they look best. Try two or three different places, leaving the plant for a week or so in each one, while you make up your mind.

SHORT CUTS

Geranium dalmaticum (right) is a tiny geranium often used in rockeries. It grows to a height of 8-10cm/3-4in and is evergreen except in the harshest winters. It can be used in any situation where larger geraniums would grow.

Harry Smith Collection

used to replace traditional herbaceous garden flowers in a miniature landscape, provided the drainage is good. Visit the rock garden section of the garden centre to find small species of pinks, artemisia and campanula, for example.

Micro-mini plants

If you are prepared to hunt them out, you can also find very unusual 'micro-miniature' species of trees and shrubs, including things like willow, birch and rowan which only grow a foot or so high.

These can be useful in very small-scale gardens, given good drainage, or in alpine gardens. These are mostly available from rock plant specialists; you can find suppliers

UNUSUAL MICRO-MINI TREES AND SHRUBS		
Betula nana 'Glengarry'	tiny twiggy birch tree	25cm/10in
Cryptomeria japonica 'Vilmoriniana'	bushy red Japanese conifer	30cm/1ft
Cytisus ardoinii 'Cottage'	cream-flowered broom	40cm/16in
Forsythia viridissima 'Bronxensis'	dwarf forsythia	30cm/1ft
Hypericum olympicum	tiny version of rose of Sharon	20cm/8in
Salix 'Boydii'	gnarled upright alpine willow	25cm/10in
Salix lanata 'Stuartii'	small willow with yellow catkins	50cm/20in
Sorbus reducta	tiny gnarled rowan, red berries, autumn tints	40cm/16in
Spiraea japonica 'Little Princess'	dwarf with pink flowers	50cm/20in
Taxus cuspidata nana	dwarf upright yew	1m/3ft
Ulmus parviflora pygmea	tiny-leaved elm, good tree shape	30cm/1ft

Forsythia viridissima 'Bronxensis' (above) is a dwarf variety of forsythia that grows to 30cm/12in. It can be grown to look like the large, well-known garden shrub.

Salix lanata 'Stuartii' (right) is a spreading, slow-growing, deciduous shrub that grows to a height of 1m/3ft. Like larger willows, it has catkins in the spring.

in a plant finder directory.

With plenty of thought and inventiveness, there is no reason why you should not miniaturize virtually any sort of garden you fancy – even water gardens and Japanese gardens. But with such specialist styles it can be very difficult – not to mention expensive – to get enough suitably sized plants and accessories with the right proportions to make even the tiniest miniature garden. So three garden styles stand out as being most practi-

cal and each is a successful candidate for miniaturization. They are the traditional formal garden, the alpine garden and the cottage garden.

Formal garden

A formal garden can look wonderful in miniature. Design it just as you would a full-sized garden, but planting compact varieties. You can have dwarf hedges, lawns, miniature trees, shrubs, border plants and annuals – even tiny topiary, all using compact versions of popular, everyday plants.

Box is probably best for low hedges and topiary – it does not mind being kept short and does not need clipping too often. For very short hedges, of around 10-15cm/4-6in, choose the edging box (*Buxus sempervirens* 'Suffruticosa').

Alpine garden

Alpines are particularly appropriate because they are naturally small and allow you to create a tiny but fascinating garden that does not need a lawn to set it off. You do not

even need a rockery as such. A scree garden is more practical to make and usually looks much more 'natural' – you can add a few nicely shaped rocks for decoration.

Grow a mixture of low carpeting plants, bun-shaped hummock plants, dwarf bulbs, tiny mountain trees and shrubs, plus dwarf conifers (small junipers do best in this situation). Ultra dwarf forms of plants such as forsythia,

A scree bed (above) with a selection of small alpine flowers and a dwarf conifer. Many alpines are naturally dwarf in size and are therefore ideal for creating a mini landscape.

Harry Smith Collection

Photos Horticultural

elm and willow are 'at home' in a mini alpine garden. They could also be used to create a mini landscape in a trough.

Cottage garden

Since roses are the backbone of a cottage garden, start your planning there, and use whichever type you choose as the basis for the scale of the rest of the planting. The smallest are miniature roses (which grow only 30-45cm/1-1½ft high), followed by patio roses (45-60cm/1½-2ft high) and then some of the smaller English roses. The latter have

been deliberately bred to look like old-fashioned roses, but flower all summer – some are only 75-90cm/2½-3ft.

There are few dwarf versions of traditional cottage garden plants. But to get the right effect you can always 'cheat' by replacing them with some of the larger and more 'cottagey' rock-garden plants.

Try dwarf artemisias (for example *A. schmidtiana* 'Nana') for silver foliage, alpine pinks and phlox varieties (more compact than the real cottage garden kind), *Leucanthemum hosmariense* for white ox-eye

GARDEN NOTES

PRUNING AND TRAINING

● Prune mini trees and shrubs lightly in late autumn to improve shape rather than reduce size. You need not aim for a conventional 'lollipop' shape – instead aim for natural craggy shapes which look more interesting.
● Conifers can be lightly clipped to shape; this looks especially good for those with strongly pyramidal or conical shapes. Conifers such as miniature pines, which have open branching shapes, can be pruned rather like large bonsai trees, by removing whole branches or parts of branches to make them look as if their shapes have been formed by the wind.
● Trees, shrubs and conifers can also be trained into shape in spring or summer by holding young branches into the required position with copper wire. Buy the special wire sold for bonsai trees. Anchor the end of the wire firmly round the trunk of the tree and twist the wire round the trunk for a few inches before reaching the branch to be trained. Continue twisting the wire round the branch, with one turn every 1cm/½in, until reaching almost the tip. Then bend the branch gently into position – do not overbend or the branch may snap. Leave the wire in place for a year.

These annual phloxes (left) are all **Phlox drummondii** *in the* **Twinkle Series.** *This group of fairly fast-growing flowers reaches a height of 15cm/6in. They bloom in summer in a wide range of colours. Even shorter species, such as* **P. caespitosa,** *are also available.*

daisy flowers, and rockery campanulas (for example, *C. carpatica*) and geraniums such as *G. sanguineum lancastriense, G. cinereum* 'Lawrence Flatman' and *G. dalmaticum*, instead of the much larger herbaceous varieties.

Use violets, sisyrinchiums, soapwort, creeping thymes and tiny sempervivums as authentic small 'fillers'.

Artemisia schmidtiana 'Nana' (left) forms a low mound of silvery-green foliage. It grows to a height of 8cm/3in with a spread of about 20cm/8in.

A tiny formal garden (right) has been created from a camomile lawn with clipped box hedges around miniature roses. This sort of self-contained area can work well as part of a larger garden.

Harry Smith Collection

Harry Smith Collection

Low-maintenance Gardening

If you are tired of spending more time working in your garden than you do relaxing in it, try replanning and replanting it on practical, labour-saving lines.

Don Wildridge

A low-maintenance garden can be just as attractive as one that takes hours of work every week – it is simply a question of how it is laid out, and the type of plants it contains. Invest a few hours in redesigning your patch, and a little labour to make the necessary changes, and you will have plenty of time to sit in a deckchair and enjoy the sight and sound of your neighbours toiling while you laze.

Trouble-free lawns

A lawn is usually the most labour-intensive part of the garden, demanding weekly mowing through the summer. It helps to reduce its size, especially by lifting odd bits and pieces, but do not be tempted to get rid of it altogether; a garden with nothing but hard surfaces can look rather bleak, especially in winter when the lawn provides the only large splash of green.

A lot of work can be saved by

Low-maintenance does not mean low interest. The combination of a lawn with conifers, shrubs and ground-cover plants (above) will provide year-round colour. Here the lawn, with its circular island bed, is the only feature that requires any regular attention.

One of the best ways to avoid work in the garden is to choose plants which perform year after year. The ground cover rose, 'Nozomi' (above) flowers in midsummer while the evergreen shrub Viburnum tinus (right) blooms in winter. Day lilies (Hemerocallis spp.) lend exotic flower shapes and a wide palette of colours to a border. The pink H. 'Cherry Cheeks' (below) is typical.

Neil Holmes

ROSE CARPETS

Ground cover roses are ideal in a low-maintenance garden, offering pretty flowers over a long period as well as suppressing weeds.

'Max Graf' has pink flowers in June-July, while the pearly pink blooms of 'Nozomi' appear in midsummer. The blood red flowers of 'Fiona' appear repeatedly.

Varieties in the 'Game bird' group are specially bred for ground cover. 'Grouse' and 'Pheasant' are pink, and 'Patridge' is white. All three are repeat flowering.

choose a rotary mower rather than a cylinder model. This will cope with grass up to a foot high without flattening it. Set the blades high and collect the cuttings in the box or by raking. They can be used as a weed-suppressing mulch on the nearest flower bed.

As a general rule, do not cut the grass too short – this only makes more work, as a scalping encourages faster growth. Leave it about 2.5cm/1in long.

Tackle the time-consuming chore of neatening the edges by eliminating them as much as possible. Remove any island beds, and have paving stones or paths running along the lawn edge wherever possible. Stop grass roots from creeping into the flower beds by digging the earth back, or by confining the lawn with corrugated plastic edging strip. An adjustable electric lawn edger is an excellent investment, useful for mowing difficult areas around trees and close to fences.

Finally, do not put fertilizer on your lawn – this makes it grow faster. Clover, daisies and other small plants can be left where they are. Get rid of large weeds like dandelions by rubbing their leaves with a touch weeder rather than by digging them out.

Hedges

Formal hedges needing close clipping, such as privet, can be hard work. If you already have

Harry Smith Collection

altering the shape of the lawn. An area with straight or gently curving edges is the easiest to mow; avoid making intricate, fussy shapes.

Make sure you have the right mower. For a small lawn, a lightweight electric mower should do the job in no more than about 20 minutes. Do not bother to use a grass box; unless the grass is very long the clippings will simply disappear into the ground and help to nourish the lawn.

If you cannot manage weekly mowing, make sure you

Neil Holmes

WATER COVER

An informal pond is very low-maintenance. The larger the area it takes up the better, as the expanse of water needs no regular attention – all you do is sit and watch the fish. Site it well away from trees, to avoid a fallen-leaf chore in autumn, and put in plenty of floating pondweed (hornwort) to oxygenate the water and keep it clear and free of blanket weed.

PERMANENT GROUND COVER

A low-maintenace garden should include plenty of evergreen ground cover to keep weeds at bay. Before planting, be sure to weed the area thoroughly, taking great care to remove deep-rooted perennials like docks or dandelions.

For cover that looks the same all year round and needs no attention, choose evergreen carpeting plants such as Japanese spurge (*Pachysandra terminalis* 'Variegata'), or any of the ivy family. These are good in shade, as are periwinkles (*Vinca* spp.), which have pretty blue flowers. There are also several prostrate conifers, such as the beautiful grey-blue *Juniperus horizontalis* 'Bar Harbor'.

Heathers make excellent ground cover in acid soil. Another acid-lover is *Cornus canadensis*, which makes an even carpet of pretty evergreen leaves topped with white flowers.

To cover an area quickly, plant rose of Sharon (*Hypericum calycinum*), whose glossy leaves set off large, long-stamened, golden flowers, or the grey-leaved snow-in-summer (*Cerastium tomentosum*). If they get too big, divide them and spread them around the garden to carry on the good work. The spring-flowering rock cresses – alyssum, arabis and aubrieta – are also evergreen, and although small at first soon form big weed-smothering clumps.

Derek Gould

one, reduce its height so there is less to be done, and invest in powerful electric hedge clippers, or spray on a growth inhibitor in late spring.

Avoid planting new hedges. Grow screens of evergreen shrubs instead, or plant a shaggy, informal hedge that is only pruned once a year. There are many suitable plants – *Viburnum tinus* gives you winter flowers if you prune in spring, and *Berberis thunbergii* 'Atropurpurea' has beautiful purple leaves that redden in autumn.

War on weeds

The constant battle against weeds is always a chore. Chemicals help to a certain extent, especially on paths and patios, where one application of a long-acting weedkiller in spring should keep them clear all year. For beds, however, a long-term, three-pronged campaign is needed.

Weed early in the year before the plants get a hold, let alone set seed. The old gardeners' saying, 'One year's seeding – seven years' weeding!' is, unfortunately, all too true.

Cover the ground with close planting so that weed seedlings get no light. Ideally, have no bare earth visible.

Mulch areas that need to be bare – around the base of rose bushes or young shrubs. Bark chippings are ideal, as they are dark brown and look very presentable, but you can also use grass cuttings, garden compost and rotted manure. Aim for a depth of about 5cm/2in to stop weed seeds germinating from below.

If things get away from you, at least cut or pull off the flower heads of weeds before they set seed, to reduce the future damage, or use a contact weedkiller. A flame gun is the weapon of last resort in such

Rose of Sharon (Hypericum calycinum, above) is a free-flowering evergreen perennial, often used for ground cover; its use here as a low hedge is exceptional. Hydrangeas are also reliable perennials. H. macrophylla 'Blue Wave' (below) produces its lace-cap blooms from mid to late summer.

Neil Holmes

Eric Crichton

avoiding tall ones, such as oriental poppies, achilleas and delphiniums, that need staking. Steer clear, too, of large-flowered dahlias or chrysanthemums, carnations and gladioli, all of which need plenty of attention and/or staking.

There is no shortage of medium-height, trouble-free perennials, but some of the best are bear's breeches (*Acanthus spinosus*), Japanese anemone (*Anemone* × *hybrida*), *Astilbe* hybrids, fleabane (*Erigeron*), hellebores, day lilies (*Hemerocallis* spp.), hostas, red hot pokers (*Kniphofia* spp.), catmint (*Nepeta mussinii*), lungwort (*Pulmonaria* spp.), leopard's bane (*Doronicum* spp.) and ice plant (*Sedum spectabile*).

Evergreens

To avoid bare soil and a bleak winter outlook, always include some flowering evergreens in a herbaceous border. Hardy specimens include the shade-loving, pink or white London pride (*Saxifraga umbrosa*), the silver-leaved, magenta-flowered lamb's ears (*Stachys lanata*), blue or white bellflower (*Campanula persicifolia*) and the low-growing, snow-white perennial candytuft (*Iberis sempervirens*).

Annuals brings welcome col-

Dark brown bark chippings make a harmoniously-coloured and effective weed-supressing mulch in borders (above).

The silver leaves of lamb's ears (Stachys lanata) are evergreen and look well with varieties of sedum (below) such as 'Autumn Joy' and low-growing 'Lidakense'.

S & O Matthews

situations. Avoid rotovators; they chop up the roots of pernicious plants like bindweed and every little bit grows.

Labour-saving plants

Trees and conifers are the most maintenance-free plants of all, as once established they need no attention whatsoever.

Flowering shrubs are also good, but choose carefully. Make sure they are hardy in your district, suitable for your soil if it is noticeably acid or alkaline, and do not require regular pruning. Allow them plenty of room to develop their full height and spread, or you will end up having to set aside time to prune them regularly to fit their space.

Displays of rare and exotic plants in garden centres can be tempting, but for low maintenance keep to tried and tested favourites like forsythia, kerria and ribes (flowering currant) for spring flowers, and lilac, philadelphus (mock orange), weigela, potentilla, deutzia and hydrangea for summer flowers. Members of the large cotoneaster genus are invaluable for evergreen leaves and bright berries.

Spring bulbs, once planted, need little work. Leave them in the ground after flowering; just remove the dead flowers, to stop seed from setting, and let the foliage wither.

Hardy perennials

A garden composed entirely of shrubs underplanted with bulbs is the most labour-saving of all, but most people like to have some hardy perennial flowering plants as well. Cut down the work here by our to the summer garden, but bedding them out can be time-consuming. Plant hardy cottage garden favourites such as love-in-a-mist, pot marigold, candytuft, godetia, gypsophila, cornflower, clarkia, larkspur and nasturtium; all will seed themselves and reappear regularly each year with no futher effort on your part.

Summer watering

Watering can be tiresome – but only if you make it so. Unless the summer is exceptionally hot and dry, it is best not to water. It takes hours to soak the ground to any depth, and sprinkling the surface merely encourages shallow root growth, making plants more vulnerable to drying out if watering is not continued. Never water a lawn. Even if the grass turns brown in the heat, it will recover amazingly quickly.

The only things that must have water are plants in containers, which dry out quickly, seedlings, and new shrubs, roses or trees that have not yet put down deep roots. Large plants benefit greatly from a mulch to stop surface evaporation. When watering them, use the spout of the can, not a rose, and give each plant a good gallon of water.

Room for roses

Most roses are hardly trouble-free, requiring careful pruning and being martyrs to aphids,

black spot and other ills, but you can still incorporate some in a low-maintenance garden.

Mulch round the base of existing bushes to conserve water and smother weeds. Spray at the first sign of aphids, before they get out of hand, and either pick off and destroy leaves afflicted with black spot, or live with it. Prune lightly, just enough to keep the bush in shape – hard pruning is done to encourage large flowers.

If buying new roses, choose shrub roses rather than hybrid teas (large-flowered bush roses), floribundas (cluster-flowered bush roses), climbers or ramblers. They can be left unpruned, and some are more resistant to disease. Look for a modern shrub rose such as 'Ballerina', whose fragrant pink flowers appear all summer, or old favourites like 'Cecile Brunner', which bears tiny pink flowers of enormous charm. Another good one is the pink-flowered rugosa 'Frau Dagmar Hartopp', considered by many experts to be the ideal rose – disease free, repeat flowering, and strongly scented, with large red hips.

Brigitte Thomas/Garden Picture Library

Derek Gould

In a small town garden, an enormous amount of work can be avoided by laying pavers or stone paths as a base for flowering perennials rather than the more traditional grass (above).

Shrub roses are the best choice for low-maintenance gardens. They do not have the large, spectacular blooms of some hybrid teas or floribundas, but they require much less attention and the best of them, such as 'Cecile Brunner' (left) bear masses of delicately coloured and scented flowers.

Patio Vegetables

Creating a mini vegetable garden in containers on a patio or another paved area in your garden is fun and full of meal appeal.

Photos Horticultural

Vegetable gardening in containers is a fascinating way to grow fresh vegetables, especially if you do not have space for a vegetable patch. It is fun, eye-catching and provides a centre of interest throughout the summer, but you should not expect to produce enough vegetables to feed your family all year round.

Range of containers
Suitable containers for vegetables include growing bags, tubs, ornamental pots, troughs, window boxes and, for certain tomato varieties, hanging baskets.

Growing bags offer an excellent way to grow tomatoes, lettuces, courgettes and beans, indeed, any crop with fibrous, shallow roots. Radishes and short-rooted carrots can also be grown in them.

Old growing bags can be rejuvenated and given a longer life by freshening up the compost. (Details of this are in Part 35).

Tubs make ideal homes for beetroot and for carrots with deep roots. Ensure that drainage holes have been drilled in the barrel's base. Line it with coarse drainage material, then add clean potting compost. If this is too expensive, use topsoil — but remember that it may be infected with a variety of pests and diseases.

Window boxes are ideal for herbs, as well as lettuces and radishes. If the box is in strong sunlight this will suit most Mediterranean-type herbs, but it will be too hot for vegetables. The limited amount of compost in window boxes and

troughs means that they must be regularly watered, or the compost will dry out and may become overheated.

Window boxes near kitchen windows are obvious homes for culinary herbs. (Suitable herbs for them are detailed in Part 24, while Part 21 reveals the techniques of growing herbs in pots.)

Clay pots look good and are suitable for vegetables such as tomatoes, which ultimately have a large amount of leafy growth. The weight of the pot has a stabilizing influence.

Large, plastic pots can also be used, but are not as stable. However, it is possible to grow tall plants in them if supporting canes are attached to

Even exotic vegetables such as aubergines (above) can be cultivated in a container or tub to add variety to family meals. Patio-grown peppers also provide a spicy addition to the cooking pot.

Photos Horticultural

firmly fixed horizontal wires.

Troughs, either supported on four legs or placed directly on the ground, are good for low-growing vegetables, as well as herbs.

Reconstructed stone containers – either pot-shaped or ornamental – are perfect for attractive herbs.

Vegetables to choose

Salad crops and herbs are ideal for containers, but you can also plant certain vegetables that are grown for their tasty roots or tubers.

Aubergines (eggplants) grow 60-90cm/2-3ft high. Three plants can keep a family of four in aubergines from midsummer to late autumn.

For success, plants need a long, hot summer and a sunny position sheltered from cold winds. Put two or three plants in a growing bag, or one in a large pot.

Either buy plants in early summer or sow seeds 3mm/⅛in deep at 18°C/64°F in mid spring. Reduce the temperature after germination, prick out seedlings when they are large enough to handle, harden them off and plant in containers when the risk of frost has passed.

Support plants in pots with

Peter McHoy

canes, or in growing bags with proprietary supports that do not pierce the bag. Keep the compost moist and nip out growing tips when plants are 25cm/10in high.

Water and feed plants regularly and harvest fruits when 10-20cm/4-8in long. Varieties to choose include 'Black Enorma' (heavy cropping), 'Black Prince' (early and heavy fruiting) and 'Elondo' (very early and dark, shiny purple).

French beans and runner beans are well suited to growing bags, as well as large pots.

The ways to success are plenty of water (but not waterlogging), sun and regular feeding.

In late spring or early summer, sow up to 12 seeds in a growing bag, pushing them 4-5cm/1½-2in into compost. Bush and dwarf runner types do not need support, but when growing climbing forms of runner or French beans, supports are essential.

Varieties to choose include 'Hammond Dwarf Scarlet' (dwarf runner, compact, heavy cropping, non-climbing), 'Gulliver' (dwarf runner, high

Aubergines (above) flourish best when the summer months are hot and dry.

Cos lettuces (right) surrounding colourful red mountain spinach (Atriplex hortensis 'Rubra') prove the point that tub-grown vegetables can be beautiful as well as exotic. French beans (below) also make a charming patio plant.

Cucumbers (below right) are perfect for growing bags although the seeds need initial protection.

yielding, self-stopping, string-less, non-climbing), 'Limelight' (bush, early, sweet) and final-ly, 'Desiree' (runner, climbing, stringless).

Beetroot is always welcome in a salad. Growing bags are usually too shallow; barrels filled with light soil are best. Use small globe varieties such as 'Monopoly' (does not need thinning; flat, round shape), 'Monogram' (does not need thinning; rich, red roots) and 'Spinel' (round, mini-roots).

Sow seeds *in situ* from early spring to early summer. Space varieties that do not need thin-ning 7.5-10cm/3-4in apart. Keep the compost moist but not saturated, as too much water can encourage an over abundance of leafy growth.

Carrots are ideal for con-tainers if short-rooted varie-ties are used, such as 'Suko' (sweet, 6cm/2½in long) and 'Kundulus' (sweet, 4-5cm/ 1½-2in long). Both are ideal for window boxes, tubs and growing bags. 'Gregory' (crisp, sweet, 7.5-10cm/3-4in long) is best in tubs.

Sow seeds 12mm/½in deep in succession, every two weeks from early spring to the end of summer. Harvest the roots as soon as they are large enough.

Courgettes are small mar-rows, harvested when 7.5-20cm/3-8in long. Plants be-come bushy and large, so choose compact varieties and plant two to a growing bag or one in a large tub.

Buy established plants dur-ing late spring or early sum-mer. Alternatively, sow seeds at 16-18°C/61-64°F in mid spring, 12mm/½in deep. Put just two seeds in a 7.5cm/3in wide pot.

After germination, reduce the temperature slightly and remove the weakest seedlings. Harden off and plant out after all risk of frost has passed.

Water and feed regularly, especially after the fruits have started to form.

A good variety to choose is 'Gold Rush' (compact, fruits can be harvested when 7.5cm/ 3in long).

Lettuces are ideal for grow-ing bags. By using several growing bags, and sowing and planting in succession, it is

COMPACT CUCUMBERS

Cucumbers are usually grown in greenhouses, where their stems are trained up and along wires. However, the variety 'Bush Champion' is non-climbing, compact and ideal for growing bags and large pots.

Towards the end of spring, open up a growing bag, water the compost and place a cloche over it so that a couple of weeks later it will be warm.

Sow seeds 12mm/ ½in deep in groups of three in three different positions in a growing bag. Place three jam jars over the seedlings, removing them after germination. When they have produced their first true leaves, thin each group to the strongest seedling.

Keep the compost moist and feed the plants after about five weeks.

BRIGHT IDEAS

Brian Carter/Garden Picture Library

Photos Horticultural

Photos Horticultural

possible to have fresh lettuces to eat from early summer to late autumn.

By growing small varieties, such as 'Tom Thumb' and the cos-type 'Little Gem', it is possible to have twelve lettuces in each growing bag. Restrict larger types to no more than eight plants.

Alternatively, oak-leaf types such as 'Salad Bowl' are an ideal choice if you have little space – individual leaves can be gathered over a long period. For extra colour on a patio, choose a red-leaved lettuce such as 'Red Salad Bowl'.

Tomatoes are always popular. They are ideal for growing bags and large pots, and can also be grown in window boxes and hanging baskets, but make sure you select the right varieties. Growing bags accommodate four plants, whereas pots about 20-25cm/8-10in wide will take one each. When planted in window boxes, set 25cm/10in apart.

Buy established plants or raise plants by sowing seeds eight weeks before planting. Sow them 3mm/⅛in deep at 18°C/64°F. After germination, reduce the temperature, prick out individually into small pots when established, then plant in a container when all risk of frost has passed.

Support plants in growing bags with proprietary frame-

works, or in pots with bamboo canes tied to horizontal wires. In window boxes, use small bush types that do not require any support.

Water and feed plants regularly. Remove any sideshoots (growths arising from leaf joints) and pinch out growing tips immediately above the set of leaves above the fourth truss. There is no need to stop bush types.

Varieties to choose include 'Pixie' (fast ripening bush type, ideal for window boxes and troughs), 'Sungold' (sweet and cherry-like, ideal for growing bags and pots), 'Tumbler' (small and cherry-like, bush-type), ideal for most hanging baskets and 'Sub Arctic Plenty' (dwarf and bushy).

Harry Smith Collection

Peter McHoy

Peter McHoy

CONTAINER SPUDS

Potatoes are a novelty crop in containers. Plant them in growing bags, or in tubs or potato barrels that allow more space for the development of tubers.

Choose an early variety such as 'Dunluce' and plant in early to mid spring. In cold areas, it may be necessary to protect emerging shoots from frost.

Plant eight tubers in a growing bag, setting them several inches deep. In large tubs or potato barrels place four or five tubers on a 10-13cm/4-5in layer of compost, and cover with about the same thickness.

As shoots appear, place more compost in the container, but do not completely cover them. Continue to cover the shoots until compost reaches the container's top, but leave a 2.5-5cm/1-2in gap for the compost to be watered.

Choose early varieties of potatoes such as 'Dunluce' for growing bags (above).

Container-grown courgettes such as 'Gold Rush' (left) are not only edible but also wonderfully ornamental.

Sowing carrots (below left) at two-weekly intervals from early spring to the end of summer will ensure a constant supply.

Ever popular tomatoes (right) are the classic container vegetable and there is a wide range of dwarf or container varieties to choose from.

Photos Horticultural

Photos Horticultural

Container Herbs

Herbs in a window box are handy for cooking but they can be much more than that, providing a fine display of flowers and colourful foliage all year.

If you want a window box that gives an attractive display of colourful flowers and foliage all year round, one filled with herbs is a good choice. It can also perfume the room every time you open the window, and will attract butterflies and provide fresh, flavourful ingredients to liven up your culinary masterpieces.

The size of the box and the fact that you still want to see out of the windows will limit the choice of plants you can grow. Tall species like fennel and tarragon are 'out', as are large bushy evergreens like bay and rosemary. But that still leaves plenty of good compact species.

Do not get carried away by visions of huge bundles of herbs drying decoratively in the rafters though. The amount of herbs you can expect to harvest from a single window box will be limited. You will get enough for weekend cooking, but if you overcut, the appearance of the window box and the health and happiness of the plants in it will certainly suffer.

Planting themes

Many people prefer to create a window box scheme from the widest mixture of herbs possible, chosen to provide a bit of everything. But because space is so limited, it is a good idea to plan a specific planting theme. This makes the box simpler to manage and will provide you with exactly what you want from the display.

If you want lots of herbs to cut for the kitchen, choose fast growing, prolific annuals such as parsley, knotted marjoram,

John Glover/Garden Picture Library

chervil and varieties of dill and coriander grown for leaf rather than seed.

If scent is the main priority, it pays to have space available indoors in the winter because some of the best subjects, like scented-leaved pelargoniums and pineapple sage, are frost tender. Take cuttings of these in late summer and keep them in trays on a windowsill indoors, replanting them outside in late spring.

For good all year round display, it is essential to include a few evergreens. Try creeping evergreen thymes and perhaps

A window box thickly planted with a range of herbs looks impressive. The varying flower and leaf colours add interest, as do the different growth habits. The plants include sage, nasturtium, lavender and strawberry.

HERB COLLECTIONS

Basils sweet basil (the most commonly seen), bush basil (small leaves, bushy habit), lettuce-leaved basil (large, crinkly leaves used to make Italian pesto sauce), 'Dark Opal' (deep reddish-purple leaves), 'Purple Ruffles' (large, frilly, purplish-red leaves), anise basil (pink flowers, aniseed-scented leaves).

Mints ginger (gold-splashed leaves), eau-de-cologne (perfumed leaves), variegated apple mint (small, round, hairy, silver-variegated leaves), spearmint (the best for mint sauce), peppermint (dark leaves, good for mint tea).

Oriental herbs perilla (used in Japanese cookery with bean curd), kemangie (lemon basil used in Indonesian cookery), coriander (leaves used in Indian cookery), Japanese parsley (celery/parsley flavour), Chinese chives (robust version of normal chives).

Thymes (*Thymus* species) Creeping evergreen: *T. serpyllum coccineus .* 'Major', *T.s.* 'Minimus' and *T.s.* 'Minus' or 'Minor'. Scented, upright: *T. fragrantissimus* (orange thyme), *T. × citriodorus* (lemon thyme), *T. herba-barona* (caraway scented). Woolly-leaved, creeping: *T. lanuginosus.*

Pat Brindley

Harry Smith Collection

The pale pink flowers and variegated leaves of Thymus vulgaris *'Silver Posie' (above) look good on their own or as part of a larger collection of thymes.*

Ginger mint (Mentha × gentilis 'Variegata') has golden-yellow leaf veins (left). It has a pungent aroma.

Three sages and two marjorams (below) provide a good contrast in foliage colours.

a tricolor sage, prostrate rosemary and dwarf lavender. These will need an annual tidy with scissors after flowering to keep them small and shapely.

You could also add a few annual flowers for extra colour in summer. Brightly coloured salvia or French marigolds team up well with red-leaved basil 'Dark Opal' (itself an annual). Or use subtler flowers like night-scented stock for scent. Sow the flower seeds directly into the box.

Single groups

If you have a special interest in a particular group of herbs, such as mints, thymes, basil or exotic oriental herbs, you can set up the window box to pro-

vide ideal conditions for them.

Mint, for instance, soon swamps other herbs in a mixed window box. By growing it alone you avoid this problem. It also takes much of the nourishment packed into the potting compost.

In a window box it needs more feeding and watering than other herbs. Tip mint out every spring, divide the plants and replace them in fresh soil-based compost.

Basils and oriental herbs, on the other hand, need very warm sheltered conditions and a dryish soil to do well.

Although most herbs prefer a warm, sunny site, if you only have a cold, shady one available you can still have a herbal

Peter McHoy

ALL YEAR COLOUR

Chives Mauve flowers attract bees.
Dwarf lavender (eg *Lavendula vera* 'Dutch') Scented flowers attract bees.
Marjoram Pink flowers attract butterflies.
Prostrate rosemary Early blue flowers.
Soapwort Pink frothy flowers in summer.
Thyme Edge boxes with creeping evergreen thymes. Bees love the midsummer flowers.
Tricolor sage Variegated cream, pink and purple edible leaves.

window box. It will be slightly unconventional but still effective. Plant up some old fashioned medicinal herbs, such as woodruff, bugle and lady's mantle. Since many of these are British native species, they also make a good 'ecological' window box.

And if space permits, why not continue the herbal theme into nearby containers at ground level? Matching window boxes and troughs, with similar planting schemes, can create a very nice rural atmosphere in even the tiniest of town courtyards.

The choice of box

Where possible choose a good sized, deep window box. Timber ones should be treated inside and out with wood preservative and allowed to dry thoroughly before planting. Line them with polythene to extend their life further.

Terracotta window boxes should be frost resistant; they are in any case heavy and need

CULINARY HERBS

Chervil Annual; resow often.
Chives Perennial; divide annually.
Coriander Annual; for leaf production choose 'Cilantro'.
Dill Annual; for leaf production choose 'Dukat'.
Knotted marjoram Treat as annual.
Parsley Treat as annual.

strong supports. Plastic window boxes should be of top quality, as cheap plastics become brittle after prolonged exposure to sunlight.

The best site for herbal window boxes is in plenty of sun, sheltered from strong winds. Given sun for less than half the day the plants will grow but will be rather leggy. In permanent shade it is vital to choose shade-tolerant species.

Buying herbs

Many herbs are readily available in garden centres. Less common varieties are available from specialist nurseries and herb farms. Check who stocks particular varieties in the current edition of a 'plant finder' directory.

Buy small plants in 8.5cm/ 3½in pots if you can. The huge pots of herbs now being sold for garden planting are too big for window box use. Make sure herb plants are fairly bushy, a good fresh green colour, and free from any obvious signs of pests or diseases.

Most herbs can be raised

from seed provided you have the space; sow in small pots on a warm window-sill indoors, then transplant to the window box. Specialist seed firms supply seeds for unusual plants such as oriental herbs.

Planting

Drill three or four drainage holes in the base of the window box if they are not already present. Cover these with concave pieces of broken clay flowerpot or with stones to prevent the compost running out through them.

A beautifully designed window box with examples of many species of herbs (top). Because the plants are generously spaced, the differences in height and the varied leaf colours and shapes can be clearly seen. A mulch on the surface keeps down weeds and enhances the look.

The leaves of variegated apple mint (above) not only look good, they also smell of apples.

Place a 2.5cm/1in layer of coarse gravel in the base of the window box if extra drainage is necessary. Then fill with a good quality John Innes (soil based) potting compost.

Pot-grown perennial herbs can be planted at any time of year, except during bad weather. Annuals are best planted in late spring or early summer, as soon as the risk of damaging frosts is past.

Some annuals which are grown for leaf production, such as chervil, basil and varieties of dill and coriander, are notoriously short-lived. You will need to re-sow seeds or replace with new plants several times during the season for continuity of cutting.

Aftercare

Check window boxes regularly to see if they need watering. Herbs will not need feeding for six to eight weeks after planting, since the compost will provide all they need. From then on, feed once a week in summer with a general purpose liquid plant feed. No feeding is necessary from mid-autumn until mid-spring.

Window boxes of annual herbs are best remade every year in spring, just before planting time. Replace the old compost with fresh material.

Boxes of mainly perennial herbs can be left for two or three years, until the plants become overgrown and need dividing or replacing with younger, neater looking specimens. Again, the best time to replant is mid to late spring.

Photos Horticultural

Pineapple sage (Salvia rutilans) has neater leaves than most sages. It looks good (above) but has no culinary uses. The leaves, however, do smell of pineapple when crushed. The plant has red flowers.

The rich purple leaves of perilla (below) contrast strongly with a collection of green-leaved herbs. The leaves have a spicy smell when bruised. This is **Perilla** *frutescens 'Atropurpurea'.*

Pat Brindley

Index

Photographic Credits

ANDREW LAWSON *15, 18, 35, 44, 55*; COLLECTIONS *7, 12, 13, 25, 71*
DAVID SQUIRE *59*; DEREK GOULD *15, 60, 64, 76, 82, 84*; DON WILDRIDGE *35, 49, 72, 74, 80, 92*
ERIC CRICHTON *7, 56, 57, 58, 59, 63, 68, 69, 70, 71, 73, 83*; EWA *40, 43*
GARDEN PICTURE LIBRARY *6, 7, 14, 19, 23, 27, 33, 34, 35, 41, 42, 60, 61, 69, 71, 84, 87, 90*
GILLIAN BECKET *16, 56, 73*; HARRY SMITH COLLECTION *19, 20, 24, 30, 38, 43, 53, 62, 66, 67, 76, 78, 79, 81, 88, 91*
INSIGHT PICTURE LIBRARY *10, 67*; MARSHALL CAVENDISH *10, 17, 19, 25, 26, 27, 59*
NEIL HOLMES *29, 81, 82*; PAT BRINDLEY *32, 50, 57, 62, 91, 93*
PETER MCHOY *9, 11, 16, 18, 21, 22, 28, 31, 37, 39, 51, 52, 65, 66, 69, 75, 86, 89, 91*
PHOTOS HORTICULTURAL *9, 15, 17, 18, 22, 23, 31, 36, 38, 41, 44, 45, 46, 47, 48, 50, 52, 53, 54, 61, 68, 72, 74, 77, 78, 85, 86, 87, 88, 89, 92, 93*; RAY DUNS *68*
S & O MATHEWS *39, 47, 48, 83*
TANIA MIDGLEY *13, 33, 36, 37, 42, 45, 46, 63*